Virgin Birth?

Virgin Birth?

*The Real Story of Mary
and Her Son Jesus*

Gerd Lüdemann

SCM PRESS LTD

Translated by John Bowden from the German
*Jungfrauengeburt? Die wirkliche Geschichte von
Maria und ihrem Sohn Jesus*, published 1997 by
Radius Verlag, Stuttgart, with additional material by
the author.

Cover: The Virgin and Child by
Botticelli (Louvre, Paris)

0 334 02724 1

First published 1998 by
SCM Press Ltd
9–17 St Albans Place London N1 0NX

Typeset by Regent Typesetting, London

Printed in Great Britain by
Biddles Ltd, Guildford and King's Lynn

This book is dedicated to
Robert W. Funk,
one of the great movers
in North American biblical studies this century

Contents

Preface

This book continues my efforts to explain the origins of the Christian religion in understandable language to men and women of today. In order to do that I have made a new translation of all the relevant ancient sources relating to the topic, and investigated them, to make it possible for readers to come to their own conclusions. As a way into the book I recommend beginning with the summary of historical events (and the diagram) on pp. 137–9 and the theological results on pp. 140–9.

Frank Schleritt co-operated closely with me in the planning and writing of the book. Without him it could not have appeared so quickly. I am grateful to Marita Hübner for her work on the parts of the book relating to feminist theology and liberation theology. Privatdozent Dr Jürgen Wehnert MA read through the manuscript critically. I thank my friend Dr John Bowden for his interest in my work and for the careful translation. My Vanderbilt colleague and friend Eugene TeSelle again read through the translation and offered valuable help. Robert Funk, the founder of the Jesus Seminar, graciously allowed me to dedicate the English edition of this book to him. Since I have added some material to it and corrected some mistakes, this book, which is being published simultaneously by SCM Press and Trinity Press International, is a new edition of the German original.

Göttingen, 29 January 1998   Gerd Lüdemann

A Note for Readers

Politically, the Protestant and Roman Catholic churches are still an important element in our state and our society. Furthermore, in almost all spheres of education and culture they and their preaching have an importance which must not be underestimated, even if this is not always clear to those directly involved. It is therefore necessary for the mental and spiritual hygiene of individuals and the positive development of democracy in Germany that the supporting pillars of the churches should also be subjected to close scrutiny. Some years ago I critically examined the resurrection of Jesus, which traditionally is regarded as *the* foundation of Christian faith; now here is a non-technical book on the Virgin Mary. I have written it because the birth of Jesus from the Virgin Mary is in many places the basic support for the assumption that Jesus is the Son of God. To this degree the miraculous birth of Jesus and his miraculous resurrection from the tomb are simply two sides of one and the same coin.

Particularly in Protestantism, in some places the virgin birth is watered down in order to defend the resurrection all the more firmly as an indispensable element in the church's lumber room. That does not change anything. It is merely the last rearguard skirmish of a faith which has become limp and weary, indeed is wasting away, but thinks that it can grasp the 'resurrection' as a last anchor of salvation. This modern Christianity is unbelieving and believing at the same time, arbitrary and self-contradictory. Indeed if one makes the additional test and asks whether according to this Christianity Jesus will ever return in judgment and whether there is a God, it is really only a name void of content. To these questions, too, the answers differ widely, ranging from censure of those who dare to put the questions to the information that God exists in becoming. Such cloudy answers must necessarily raise even more questions.

I have recently been criticized by this modern circle, which always wants to be up with the times, for being an Enlightenment fundamentalist or a historical fundamentalist, for slashing and burning religion and always sowing only doubt. The aim of this criticism is to disqualify me. Now 'the capacity to doubt and especially to sustain this doubt over a long period' is 'one of the rarest things on this planet. In truth human beings are mammals who cannot take uncertainty at all well and have a deep longing for firm convictions' (Reik 1927: 382). Precisely because our human nature is created in this way and cannot bear existence without illusions, I happily accept the taunt of historical or Enlightenment fundamentalism. I would rather live in a house built on solid foundations than in a priestly castle in the air. One gets the impression that the criticism I have mentioned simply wants to paint over the weaknesses of its own faith and in so doing presupposes that theology – like a magician – must do away with doubt (cf. Hirsch 1989: 13). Those who talk of radical historical criticism slashing and burning religion should clarify their own foundations without delay if they are not to incur the charge of having an airy-fairy longing for faith. Historical criticism has a vitally important contribution to make, particularly in investigating the foundations of faith, because it first of all works out what the first Christians really believed. In doing this, historical criticism has the task of demystifying the world, in order to pave the way for peace between men and women of different faiths, a peace which the great religions, including their sub-groups, have not made possible. Indeed, over recent centuries they have done everything in their power to prevent it. First of all, it should be noted that in Europe the wars of religion between Catholics and Protestants were not ended as a result of better insights, but were resolved by the hand of the secular state. In other words, it was only the discovery and application of reason that could prevent the two churches, which allegedly have the same Lord, from tearing each other apart.

So even today the requirement is to make peace through enlightenment. The consequence of this requirement for scholarly theology is that it should persist in demystifying the foundations of faith in order to lay a better foundation – and to hold Christian faith to its claim that the divine Word, Jesus Christ, became flesh. Those who do not devote all their strength to this task within theology and the church would do better to state openly that the historical facts are unimportant. But such a position unavoidably leads to a religious fundamentalism which breaks with a readiness for dialogue, a capacity for criticism and openness. It leaves the ground of modernity, in which for Christians, too, the problem of history has become the fateful question.

At present there are two ways of avoiding the dilemma mentioned. The *first* is for pastors calmly to be ordained to something that they need no longer believe. This way is evidently favoured by leading church officials, who are predominantly concerned with preserving existing structures. For example, they even encourage discussions on the validity of the Apostles' Creed, but without a thought of doing away with it. The slogan seems to be, 'When the children have shouted themselves hoarse, we can get back to the order of the day and leave everything as it was.' Recently I wrote in a church paper:

Do away with the creed? What a hypothetical discussion! Within our churches it is carried on only on condition that the creed is never buried. Those who dare to discuss the question in a purely academic way are like figures in a sandpit, the wooden frame of which is carefully protected by the church governments. The scale is established: if the figures became human and thus grew out of the sandpit, the rules of the game would be broken.

But the situation is very serious: in the confusion of interpretations what we really believe remains obscure.

Some understand 'risen from the dead' as a historical event; others do not want the resurrection to be viewed in this particular way. However, they immediately add that the image of the resurrection makes an indispensable statement which is vital for Christian faith. But what is the foundation for this image if Jesus demonstrably died and did not rise? Here, as in all the other articles of the creed, there is a tremendous need for clarification.

I want to understand and therefore to know what I believe. Here it is not a matter of interpretations and provisionalities, but of the ultimate questions. We live only once and need to know what life is about. To live means to engage in a venture, to let go and push out from the safe bank, to venture into the unknown. It also means saying no and bidding farewell to the familiar barriers of thought.

But the mental block is made of different material from the plank in the eye: perhaps people do not even sense the latter. However, although the board presses, it nevertheless seems necessary. It is affirmed in a sanctimonious way precisely because it blocks curiosity, the thirst for knowledge and even the longing for life itself (*Der Sonntagsblatt*, 7/14 February 1997).

I have often got to know the *other* way of dealing with the dilemma mentioned above in conversations with women pastors and committed Christian women in the church. They point out that the church takes place at the grass roots and that 'church' must not be identified with 'church government'. At the grass roots the artificial problems of dogmatics no longer arise, and the question of the literal understanding of the virgin birth and the resurrection have long been superseded.

I do not share this optimism. It is naive, far too generous and, as experience shows, unprotected from the church government. For how many women have been elevated to positions in church government over the last twenty years? How many of the undogmatic positions of the grass roots find an echo, for example, in the official statements of the Protestant church? Where in church government are real spokesmen for grass-roots women to be found?

Therefore I can only regard both ways as evasive manoeuvres in the face of a hopeless dilemma which can be formulated like this. A faith is confessed in the church, the main elements of which have been refuted historically once and for all, from the birth of Jesus from a virgin to his alleged resurrection from the tomb. In the long run it is an intolerable situation for believers to be robbed of their historical foundation and to be allowed to understand everything only in a figurative sense, while nevertheless repeating the creed word for word every Sunday. Here we need a fundamental remedy which overcomes the present state of hypocrisy and creates a viable foundation. The presupposition for this remedy is one's own confession that what is dead is dead and that all the attempts to revive the foundations of faith mentioned above are in vain.

Here any scholarly denial is a positive intellectual act which prepares the way for the new. But the threat is that the new will be prevented from growing by the rubble of the church tradition. It is therefore time to lift the virgin veil which – woven from a mixture of dogmatics, piety and fantasy – has lain over the figure of Mary. To anticipate my proposal, Mary is better unveiled, because in this way she becomes more credible and more human. The same applies to early Christianity and Christianity in general. It gains everything if it appears without a veil. Only then does it succeed in rising from emasculated church dogmatics into the fertile sphere of life which is sometimes chaotic but in the end is shining, warm and beautiful.

Introduction

Stocktaking

Protestant confusion

Every Sunday, most Christians in all the churches in the world confess as they recite the Apostles' Creed that Jesus was born of the virgin Mary. Now, as was mentioned in the introduction, modern Christians completely discount the historicity of the virgin birth and understand it in a figurative sense. A few typical examples, all from renowned contemporary German systematic theologians, may serve as evidence for this. Wilfried Joest writes:

> 'The question whether it [viz., the virgin birth] is really about the fact of a real sign given by God or (what seems . . . more probable to me) is a *symbolic* sign for the mysterious origin of Jesus which grew up in the thought of early Christians, should be left open . . . Even if it is only a symbolic sign, it retains its meaning for faith as an expression of the truth that Jesus is the "only-begotten" son, who did not come into being through human possibility but came to us through the will and the action of God' (Joest 1989: 241).

Criticism: the distinction between real and symbolic sign does not do justice to the biblical texts about the virgin birth. Thus when her pregnancy is announced, Mary asks, 'How can this be, since I do not know a man (i.e. have not had sexual intercourse with a man)?' The answer of the angel Gabriel states that the normal procreation of a child by a man has been dispensed with: (No man will sleep with you and impregnate you, but) 'holy spirit will come upon you and power of the Most High will overshadow you' (Luke 1.35). That is meant really, and not in a metaphorical sense.

Wolfgang Pannenberg remarks:

> '. . . the Christian can very well assent to the intention which prompted the story of Jesus' virgin birth, even if this intention has grown beyond the expression it found in the nativity legend to the idea of the pre-existence of the sonship of Jesus in the eternal nature of God. Moreover the Christian today can also share the intention which allowed this formula to be absorbed into the creed. In the first place the point was to show that the Son of God is really identical with the historical person, Jesus of Nazareth . . . This goes together with the second point, that Jesus did not only become Son of God at some particular point of time during his lifetime, but was, and is, in his person from the very beginning the only Son of God, mankind's mediator of the sovereignty of God. Seen in this light, the formula of the virgin birth is an expression of the final nature of the revelation of God in Jesus, of God's bond with this man, and through him with mankind' (1972: 76f.).

The question whether the intention postulated by Pannenberg is identical with the one which has arisen from the story of the virgin birth may be left aside here. At all events it is certain that Pannenberg can only be said to be inconsistent in continuing to confess the virgin birth which even he terms unhistorical. And he himself seems to realize something of this inconsistency when he continues: 'For the alternative would be, not to alter this particular formulation alone, but the whole creed in general. But it is only in the classic form it has acquired that the creed is the sign of the unity of Christianity throughout history' (77).

Wilfried Härle turns things upside-down. First, he argues that the doctrine of the virgin birth can lead to Jesus Christ appearing as a kind of demigod, who is neither truly human nor truly God (1995: 349). Secondly, it can be misunderstood to mean 'that human sexuality must be excluded in order to make it possible to describe the divine (and thus sinless) origin of Jesus Christ. But that would bring human sexuality so dangerously near to sin that its creatureliness and thus its given natural nature can hardly still be perceived in a dispassionate way' (350).

In his view it is these theological objections – 'and not the scientific and medical objections which could similarly be thought of' (sic!) – which are the 'main reasons why the doctrine of the virgin birth is to be judged problematical, indeed dangerous' (ibid.). Härle continues:

'But despite this danger it does *not* seem to me right to declare that the confessional form "conceived by the Holy Spirit, born of the virgin Mary" is "finished". In fact it points to a problem which calls for theological consideration and contains a noteworthy indication of the solution of this problem. However, that is the case only if talk of the virgin birth, like all other statements concerning the reality and nature of God, is recognized and acknowledged as *metaphorical* discourse . . . In the virgin birth the human participation [viz. in the incarnation] is not excluded or ruled out, but is limited to acceptance and conception . . . the specifically *male* nature of the involvement (which, however, is in no way limited to men) is thus excluded by talk of the virgin birth as unsuitable for the mystery of the divine origin of Jesus Christ, though this in no way excludes the human participation' (350f.).

For the symbolic-metaphorical reinterpretation of the virgin birth practised in all these views see the general comment by Christoph Türcke:

3

'Each time the method is the same: the dogmatic statements are divided into those which one can still accept as
valid currency and those which are better taken metaphorically. Here, however, the criterion is not the intrinsic
logic which once made the interconnection of dogmas a
first-rate intellectual structure but the question of what
modern men and women still want or do not want to
identify with. Thus for example the saving action of God
and the redeeming death of Christ are put in the little bag
of facts, and the virgin birth and the devil in the crop of
metaphors' (1992, 67).

The power of liturgy and its consequences

If we compare the official statements of the Evangelical
Church in Germany with these views, the situation proves to
be rather different. The unhistorical character of the virgin
birth is never a topic in statements about Mary. For example,
an examination of the episcopal statements made last
Christmas showed that at no point was the virgin birth
narrated in the Bible said to be unhistorical. Further evidence
confirms this impression. The liturgy and hymns, especially at
Christmas, clearly, emphatically and unmistakably emphasize the virginity of Mary and thus cement her unique, virgin
role in Christian faith. However many arguments the
Christian may hear against it and seriously consider in
religious education or even in confirmation classes, these are
again qualified, if not dismissed, in the rituals and liturgies of
worship.

We need only turn to the most popular Christmas hymns
and carols to see the central role given to the virginity of
Mary. They impressively demonstrate the dogmatic phantom
world into which the normal Christian is conscripted when
taking part in worship. The hymns and carols I quote here
are so familiar that no specific reference need be given:

'O Come, All Ye Faithful'

'God of God, light of light,
Lo, he abhors not the virgin's womb.'

'Hark, the Herald Angels Sing'

'Late in time behold him come,
Offspring of a virgin's womb.'

'Christians, awake'

'With them the joyful tidings first begun
Of God incarnate and the Virgin's son.'

'A great and mighty wonder'

'The Virgin bears the infant
with virgin honour pure.'

'A Virgin Most Pure'

'A virgin most pure, as the prophets forthtell,
Hath brought forth a baby, as it has befell.'

Common features and their damaging consequences

Furthermore, for a long time there has been a tacit agreement between the two great churches in Germany that as far as possible they should show a common front in public. Well-known examples of this are the 'Statement of the Council of the Evangelical Church in Germany and the German Conference of Bishops on the Economic and Social Situation in Germany', entitled *Towards a Future in Solidarity and Justice*, published in 1997, and the 'Week for Life' (1–7 June 1997), which is deliberately focussed on a German public. The accumulation of these joint approaches leads to the two churches being seen as one group. As a result, for example the public transfers the Roman Catholic Church's doctrine of Mary in full to its Protestant partner. The unwelcome consequence is that people also leave the Protestant church because they no longer agree with particular Roman Catholic doctrines – and that applies to a special degree to those relating to the virgin Mary.

The ecumenical situation

In addition, the ecumenical situation needs to be kept in mind. Representatives of the Russian Orthodox Church are left speechless when they note the historical-critical work done in the Western churches and the consequences which are drawn from it. In particular neither the ordination of women nor the evaluation of homosexuality, which is no longer just negative, can ever be accepted by the Russian Orthodox side. Therefore at present (1997) about forty per cent of Russian Orthodox bishops are hostile to ecumenism. Furthermore, for the Orthodox Church there is no doubt that Jesus rose physically, and of course Mary remained a perpetual virgin.

Now German Protestantism is committed to the ecumenical idea, the notion of the unity of all Christians. The umbrella organization of German Protestants, the Evangelical Church in Germany (EKD), finances – roughly – almost half the domestic budget of the World Council of Churches (WCC), more than twice the contribution of its Protestant partner churches in the USA (see the figures in Besier 1997: 61). But the majority of member churches of the WCC, loyal to the Christian tradition, understand the virgin birth in a literal sense. Therefore it is not surprising that leading representatives of the EKD do not make the virgin birth of Jesus from Mary a topic of discussion, despite clear historical facts and despite their own better insight, and prefer to keep quiet about the truth.

The way forward

In view of the Protestant confusion described above and the precarious ecumenical situation it is not surprising that the uninitiated observer no longer knows what is taught in the churches about the virgin birth and what Christians (should) really believe.

In order to achieve clarity on this point, first, as part of the introduction, I shall describe the way in which Martin Luther and the confessional writings of the Evangelical Lutheran Church understand Mary (for the confessional writings see the bibliography, *Bekenntnisschriften, etc.* = BSLK). Then I shall turn to the traditional Roman Catholic teaching about Mary, describe Catholic piety focussed on Mary and after a survey of more recent Protestant evaluations of Mary formulate the historical task of this book.

Mary in Martin Luther and in the Lutheran confessional writings

Martin Luther

According to Luther's *Commentary on Psalm* 22.10 ('You took me from my mother's womb') of 1513 or 1516, Jesus Christ was taken from the womb of Mary and received in that of the Father. This taking happened without any violation of nature and at the same time revealed her impotence to bring forth such a son (cf. WA 3, p.136).

In his exegesis of Isa.7.14 ('Behold, the *almah* is pregnant and will bear a son, whom she will call Immanuel'), Luther attached special importance to the interpretation of the Hebrew word *almah* in the sense of *bethulah* (= virgin; cf. WA 11, pp.322f.) Therefore he defended Mary's virginity and was ready to pay one hundred florins to anyone who demonstrated that *almah* did not mean virgin but young woman (cf. WA 53, p.634). This proof has meanwhile been given: Luther would have had to pay up (cf. Luz 1992: 107).

In his *Exposition of the Magnificat* (= Luke 1.46–55) of 1521, Luther unequivocally states that the holy virgin Mary 'became a mother in a supernatural way, with her virginity intact' (cf. WA 7, p.549). The 'tender mother of God' may be regarded as a shining example of a Christian life which consists wholly in faith and God's grace.

Luther's *Lesser Catechism* (1529) mentions the virgin birth in the article about redemption (as does the *Greater Catechism* of the same year). However, the subsequent exposition does not go into it. The reason for this is that the virgin birth needed no explanation. It was taken for granted.

In Luther's *Schmalkald Articles* (1537), the first part of the article in the christological section reads: 'That the son is thus born human, that he is conceived of the Holy Spirit without human involvement and born of the pure, holy virgin Mary' (BSLK, p.414).

Luther also affirmed the expression 'mother of God' approved by the Council of Ephesus in 431. In his view the Council did not state anything new in the faith, but merely defended the old faith. For this article had been present in the church from the beginning (cf. WA 50, pp. 590f.). (For Luther, see the survey in Grass 1991: 44–57.)

The Lutheran confessional writings

The writings of Luther mentioned above, the Lesser and Greater Catechisms and the Schmalkald Articles, are also part of the confessional writings of the Evangelical Lutheran Church. Their understanding of the virgin birth therefore need not be repeated here. We shall simply look at three further documents from the Lutheran confessional writings: the Augsburg Confession and the Apology for it, and the Formula of Concord.

The *Augsburg Confession*, composed by Philipp Melanch-thon in 1530, quite naturally takes over the doctrine of the virgin Mary and the virgin birth of Christ where reference is made to the creed of the early church. Article II teaches 'that God the Son became man, born of the pure virgin Mary' (BSLK, p.54).

The 1531 *Apology for the Augsburg Confession*, also from the pen of Philipp Melanchthon, does not contain any statement about the virgin birth. By contrast, in Article XXII ('On the invocation of the saints') there is a criticism of the cult of Mary. With reference to a formula of absolution current at that time ('The passion of our Lord Jesus Christ, the merits of the most blessed Virgin Mary and all the saints shall be to you for the forgiveness of sins') and a prayer ('Mother of graces, preserve us from the enemy, accept us in the hour of death'), Melanchthon writes:

'However much we, too, grant that the blessed Mary prays for the church – does she herself accept souls in death? Does she conquer death, does she make them alive? What does Christ do if blessed Mary does that? Even if she, too, is most worthy of the highest honours, she does not will to be made equal to Christ, but rather that we should have her exemplary acts in view and comprehend them. But experience itself confirms that in the public view the blessed Virgin has wholly taken the place of Christ. People invoke her, trust in her mercy, want to be reconciled with Christ through her, as if Christ were not the reconciler but only the terrible judge and avenger . . . But we know that Christ's merits alone are reconciliation for us . . . So one may not trust that we will be held righteous through the merits of the blessed Virgin or the other saints' (BSLK, pp.322f.; the original text is in Latin).

The *Formula of Concord* of 1577, the last part of the confessional writings, on the basis of which all Lutheran pastors are still ordained, makes the following statement about the Virgin Mary:

'For the sake of this personal union and communion of the natures (= the divine and human nature of Jesus Christ), Mary, the highly praised virgin, gave birth not to a mere man but to such a man as is truly the Son of God the Most High, as the angel attests: who also showed his divine majesty in his mother's womb, by being born of a virgin without violation of her virginity; therefore she remained truly Mother of God and nevertheless a virgin' (BSLK, p.1024).

In other words, this confessional writing not only teaches the virgin birth but, like Martin Luther, explicitly states that Mary's hymen remained intact during birth. The official Lutheran confession is much nearer on this point to the Roman Catholic doctrine of Mary than is generally recognized.

Mary in Roman Catholic doctrine

There are four articles of faith relating to Mary which are binding on Catholics:

1. the divine motherhood,
2. the perpetual virginity,
3. the immaculate conception and
4. the bodily assumption of Mary.

We shall investigate these points in order and in each case indicate what is said about the individual questions by *The Catechism of the Catholic Church* published in 1993 (in English in 1994). It is also natural to do this because in this document from the highest papal circles the Catholic faith has been presented for a wide public. The large number of copies printed and the dissemination in all modern languages might be taken as an eloquent sign of the general validity of the catechism. So the sentences quoted below in fact reflect present-day Catholic belief in Mary, the mother of Jesus. For a comparison, after each extract I shall look briefly at the Reformation teaching of the sixteenth century and that of the Greek Orthodox Church of the present day. I am doing this in order to investigate what the three great churches have in common.

1. Divine motherhood

Catechism of the Catholic Church, 466:
'. . . Christ's humanity has no other subject than the divine

10

person of the Son of God, who assumed it and made it his own, from his conception. For this reason the Council of Ephesus proclaimed in 431 that Mary truly became the Mother of God by the human conception of the Son of God in her womb: "Mother of God, not that the nature of the Word or his divinity received the beginning of its existence from the holy Virgin, but that, since the holy body, animated by a rational soul, which the Word of God united to himself according to the hypostasis, was born from her, the Word is said to be born according to the flesh."'

495: 'Called in the Gospels "the mother of Jesus", Mary is acclaimed by Elizabeth, at the prompting of the Spirit and even before the birth of her son, as "the mother of my Lord". In fact, the One whom she conceived as man by the Holy Spirit, who truly became her Son according to the flesh, was none other than the Father's eternal Son, the second person of the Holy Trinity. Hence the Church confesses that Mary is truly *"Mother of God" (Theotokos)*.'

Jesus Christ was really God and really human. Since his birth is to be regarded as the birth of the incarnate God, then logically the mother of Jesus must be called the mother of God. Conciliar fathers approved this thesis for the first time in Ephesus in 431 and officially confirmed the expression 'mother of God' with the following harsh words: 'Anyone who does not confess that the Immanuel (cf. Matt. 1.23) is in truth God and therefore the holy virgin is mother of God because she has given birth according to the flesh to the incarnate Word which comes from God, let him be anathema' (DS 252). The Reformers never put this decision of the Council of Ephesus in question (see the previous section). It is still also explicitly endorsed by the Greek Orthodox Church.

According to present-day Roman Catholic mariology, the role of Mary in the birth of Jesus was an active one. An involuntary conception would be an incomplete conception, and this would entail an incomplete motherhood. It is said that Mary's reply to the angel, 'Be it to me as you have said' (Luke 1.38) is an expression of her readiness to conceive in both a physical and a spiritual sense. For instance, Roman Catholic mariologists teach that Mary first conceived her son Jesus with her soul through faith before the conception took place in her womb. This is doubtless a logical view if one understands Luke 1.38, the text just quoted, literally. The angel Gabriel had announced to Mary: 'Behold, you will become pregnant and give birth to a son, and you shall give him the name Jesus' (Luke 1.31). When Mary asks how that can happen because she has not had sexual intercourse, the angel replies, 'Holy Spirit will come upon you, and the power of the Most High will overshadow you . . .' (Luke 1.35). Thereupon Mary is ready to conceive as 'handmaid of the Lord', and the story takes its well-known course.

2. Perpetual virginity

Catechism of the Catholic Church, 499:
'The deepening of faith in the virginal motherhood led the Church to confess Mary's real and perpetual virginity even in the act of giving birth to the Son of God made man. In fact, Christ's birth "did not diminish his mother's virginal integrity but sanctified it". And so the liturgy of the Church celebrates Mary as *Aeiparthenos,* the "Ever-virgin".'

500: The brothers and sisters of Jesus are to be understood as his close relatives.

501: 'Jesus is Mary's only son, but her spiritual motherhood extends to all men whom indeed he came to save: "The Son whom she brought forth is he whom God placed as the first-born among many brethren, that is, the faithful in whose generation and formation she co-operates with a mother's love (LG 63)."'

These statements presuppose three things:

(a) Mary was a virgin before she conceived Jesus, and the conception took place without male fertilization and therefore without damaging Mary's hymen (= before birth, Latin *ante partum*).

(b) Mary remained virgin during the birth of Jesus: in the process of birth, when the child went through the natural channels of Mary's body and came into the world, her hymen remained intact (= at birth: Latin, *in partu*).

The authors of the *Catechism* presuppose in paragraph 499 that Mary's virginity could have been *diminished* by the birth of Jesus. Therefore they also make a biological statement. Certainly Catholic theologians of the present twist and turn over this point and allow themselves to be celebrated as heroes of honesty when, like Karl Rahner (1962) and Hans Küng (1992), they allow a symbolic interpretation of this dogma laid down at the Council of Constantinople in 553 and thus of the birth of Jesus from the virgin Mary. Honesty on this point – that remains no more than a fig-leaf when the same theologians, for example, although they know better, inexorably hold to the bodily resurrection and in general think that human beings may not and cannot put any limits to the workings of God. Beyond doubt that is thoroughly biblical (cf. Luke 1.37: 'For with God nothing is impossible') and obvious if one bases it on the scholastic statement: 'God could do it, it was fitting, and so he did it' (*Deus potuit, decuit, igitur fecit*). However, here we are not dealing with the necessities of dogma but with historical probabilities, which are taken to be *true* until new arguments are advanced for other probabilities.

So however many tricks are used, they cannot change the binding testimony of the *Catechism of the Catholic Church* that the dogma of the perpetual virginity of Mary also has a biological side and continues to stand despite individual attempts at mediation.

(c) Mary had no other children after Jesus; and although she was married to Joseph, she did not have sexual intercourse with him (= after birth: *post partum*).

Here, too, it must be noted that the Reformers in the sixteenth century agreed with this Roman Catholic doctrine.

Thus, as was demonstrated above, at the time of the Reformation the name 'ever-virgin' was already almost a second name for Mary. It was so widespread that even Martin Luther and his followers used it, without discussing its presuppositions further. But when they came to speak about it, they too were utterly convinced that the birth of Jesus took place without damage to Mary's hymen, which remained intact even afterwards.

According to Greek Orthodox teaching Jesus had only cousins (no brothers). The womb of the mother of God is a holy temple. A well-known Greek Orthodox hymn says: 'Foreign to mothers is virginity and virgins do not give birth; with you, Mother of God, both these things came to pass. Therefore we praise you together with all the peoples of the earth.'

3. Immaculate conception

Catechism of the Catholic Church, 491:
'Through the centuries the Church has become ever more aware that Mary, "full of grace" through God, was redeemed from the moment of her conception. That is what the dogma of the Immaculate Conception confesses, as Pope Pius IX proclaimed in 1854:

"The most Blessed Virgin Mary was, from the first moment of her conception, by a singular grace and privilege of almighty God and by virtue of the merits of Jesus Christ, Saviour of the human race, preserved immune from all stain of original sin."'

492: 'The "splendour of an entirely unique holiness" by which Mary is "enriched from the first instant of her conception" comes wholly from Christ: she is "redeemed, in a more exalted fashion, by reason of the merits of her Son". The Father blessed Mary more than any other created person "in Christ with every spiritual blessing in the heavenly places" and chose her "in Christ before the foundation of the world, to be holy and blameless before him in love".'

493: 'The Fathers of the Eastern tradition call the Mother of God "the All-Holy" *(Panagia),* and celebrate her as "free from any stain of sin, as though fashioned by the Holy Spirit and formed as a new creature". By the grace of God Mary remained free of every personal sin her whole life long.'

The doctrine of the immaculate conception does not refer to the birth of Jesus, as is wrongly often assumed, but to the birth of Mary from her mother Anne. (Martin Luther had made a vow to Anne near Erfurt in 1505 that he would become a monk.) Mary as the lodging place of the son of God must already have been conceived without sin – thus the inner logic of this doctrinal statement, which came to be recognized only gradually after the fourteenth century and was disputed by such a normative theologian as Thomas Aquinas (1225–1274): Mary 'must have been conceived in original sin, for her conception was the work of sexual union . . . Now sexual union, which after the sin of our first ancestor cannot take place without sinful pleasure, introduced original sin into the child' *(Comp.theol.*224).

The Reformers of the sixteenth century were opposed to the dogma of the Immaculate Conception as it was not contained in scripture. In their view, Mary, too, was subject to original sin.

The Greek Orthodox Church in fact knows the feast of the Conception of Anne (9 December); however, at it the emphasis is not on the 'immaculate conception' but on the fact that Mary's parents, Joachim and Anne, could produce life despite their age. Moreover the Greek Orthodox Church, like the church of the Reformation, sees Mary as being completely on the human side: she has to die because she has sinned. As Paul wrote in Rom.3.23: human beings 'have all sinned and all fall short of the praise they should have with God'.

4. Bodily assumption

Catechism of the Catholic Church, 966:

'Finally the Immaculate Virgin, preserved free from all stain of original sin, when the course of her earthly life was finished, was taken up body and soul into heavenly glory, and exalted by the Lord as Queen over all things, so that she might be the more fully conformed to her Son, the Lord of lords and conqueror of sin and death.' The Assumption of the Blessed Virgin is a singular participation in her Son's Resurrection and an anticipation of the resurrection of other Christians.'

The *Catholic Catechism* sums this up in a brief text in §974:

'The Most Blessed Virgin Mary, when the course of her earthly life was completed, was taken up body and soul into the glory of heaven, where she already shares in the glory of her son's resurrection, anticipating the resurrection of all members of his body.'

The dogma of the bodily ascension of Mary was proclaimed in 1950 and of course does not find any assent in the present-day Greek Orthodox Church. There the most important feast in the church calendar on 15 August is called the 'Dormition of the Mother of God'. The sixteenth-century Reformers also rejected this dogma. Pope Pius XII's Bull concluded by stating:

'. . . we proclaim, declare and define that it is a divinely revealed dogma that the immaculate Mother of God, the perpetual virgin Mary, after she ended her earthly life, was taken up body and soul into heavenly glory' (DS 3903).

According to this dogma, immediately after the end of her life the body of Mary was transformed into the heavenly body and thus translated to heaven. How that could have happened is not explained. Even the death of Mary is not

16

discussed. This is often overlooked. However, it remains to be noted that according to the wording of the Bull the reception into heaven simply takes place after the ending of Mary's earthly life. For this reason, some say that Mary did not die at all. Others think that she died, but that her body did not decay and was immediately reunited with her soul after the resurrection from death (cf. e.g. Børresen 1988, 79f.). So far these questions have yet to be given a final answer, and present-day Roman Catholic theologians in fact continue to discuss the matter earnestly – an example of the way in which fantastic games are played and castles built in the air on the basis of particular presuppositions which are demonstrably misleading (why 'progressive' Protestants are not above such criticism is explained on pp. 28–39 below).

Results

The texts of the four binding Catholic doctrines about Mary in the present, cited above, speak for themselves. Anyone who studies them attentively will immediately recognize that they are false, vain and in some respects even deceptive for enquiring men and women. They heighten the significance of Mary almost without limit. So it is an irony of the utmost magnitude that in the twentieth century, of all centuries, the bodily assumption of Mary has been elevated to a dogma. One could almost say: the greater the serious objections to traditional faith, the greater the folly of dogmatics and the church.

Mary in Roman Catholic piety

However, we can only understand this process if we note the importance of Mary in art (cf. the impressive selection in Chadwick 1990 and Pelikan 1996), and above all in Catholic piety. Here the manifold appearances of the Mother of God play a role which can hardly be overestimated, though – it should be remarked first by way of qualification – despite defensive assertions to the contrary (cf. Laurentin 1961), there is no *scientific* documentation (cf. generally Rahner 1963). So here *a priori* we find ourselves on shaky ground. However, we must nevertheless attempt to hack a path through the jungle of luxuriant private and popular piety.

In going on to quote relatively extensively from the reports of two women, Elisabeth von Schönau and Anna Katharina Emmerick, my intention is to give a general impression of appearances of Mary. We have only brief testimonies to the famous appearances of Mary to others, and here from the beginning the formation of legends is even more rampant (cf. Rahner 1963: 9).

The appearances of Mary to Elisabeth von Schönau

Elisabeth von Schönau (1129–1164) did not just experience countless appearances of Christ. She also often saw Mary. Of noble origin, at the age of twelve she entered the Benedictine convent of Schönau. Elisabeth was frequently sick, and her ecstasies were often accompanied by painful attacks. Her brother, Ekbert von Schönau, collected her notes, and in the process, as is evident at some points, also introduced his own thoughts and interests.

In one of her visions Elisabeth saw the resurrection of Mary from the tomb and her welcome into heaven:

'In the year in which the book of the ways of God was proclaimed to me by the angel of the Lord, on the day on which the church celebrates the octave of the Assumption of our Lady, at the hour of worship I was in a rapture of the spirit, and she, my comforter, the mistress of heaven, appeared to me in her fashion.

Then I asked her as I had previously been admonished by one of our elders and said, "My Lady, may it be pleasing to your Benevolence to vouchsafe to grant us information as to whether you were taken up into heaven only in the Spirit or also in the flesh."

I said this because, as they say, the statements about this in the books of the fathers are doubtful.

And she said to me, "What you ask, you cannot yet know. But it shall be that this will be revealed through you."

Therefore for the whole period of this year I did not dare to inquire further about it either of the angel who is familiar to me or of her when she showed herself to me. But that brother (= Ekbert) who urged me to this enquiry gave me some prayers with which I was to ask of her the revelation that she had promised me. And when after the course of a year the feast of her Assumption returned, I was weak from a sickness lasting many days, and as I was lying in bed at the time of worship, with great effort I entered a rapture of the spirit. And I saw in a far distant place a tomb bathed in much light and something like a woman's figure in it, and around it stood a great crowd of angels. And after a moment she was raised from the tomb and together with that crowd of bystanders was raised to the heights. And as I looked up, behold, there came to her from the heavenly heights a man transformed beyond all imagining; in his right hand he bore a sign of a cross on which a banner also appeared. I recognized that he was the Lord and Saviour himself and an infinite host of angels was with him. And receiving her thus with joy they took her with a great chorus into the heavenly heights. And when I had seen this, after a short time my Lady came to the portal of light in which I usually see her, stood there, and showed me her transfiguration.

At the same hour the angel of the Lord was with me . . . and I said to him, "My lord, what is the meaning of this great vision which I saw?"

And he said, "It has been shown you in a vision how Our Lady was taken up into heaven both in the flesh and in the spirit"' (Dinzelbacher 1989: 101–3).

Later Elisabeth reports how Mary told her that all the

apostles of the Lord had been present at her burial. 'All were there and committed my body to the earth with great reverence' (ibid., 105).

The appearances of Mary to Anna Katharina Emmerick

Secondly, mention should be made of the appearances of Mary to the stigmatized Augustinian nun Anna Katharina Emmerick (1774–1824), which became famous through the literary treatment of them by the convert Clemens Brentano (1778–1842). Their effect even now can hardly be over-estimated. Anna Katharina Emmerick reports how she saw the young Mary and her mother Anne:

'Yesterday evening, when I had prayed and had barely got to sleep, a person came to my bedside. I recognized her as a maiden whom I had often seen previously. She spoke quite briefly to me: "Today you have spoken much of me, now you shall also see me, so that you do not err over me." I asked her, "Have I spoken too much?"

She replied briefly, "No!", and disappeared. She was still in a virgin state, and was slim and attractive; her head was covered with a white cap which reached down to her neck, where it was drawn together into a point, as thought it was binding up her hair. Her long garment, which covered her completely, was of white wool, and the sleeves attached seemed to be gathered somewhat roughly only at the elbows. Above it she wore a long coat of brown wool like camel hair.

Hardly had I rejoiced at the contact with this appearance than suddenly an aged woman in similar clothing with a somewhat more bowed head and very sunken cheeks came to my bedside. She was like a beautiful old Jewish woman, gaunt, and around fifty-five. I thought, "Well, what does this old Jewish lady want with me?" Then she said to me: "You need not be afraid, I simply want to show you how I was when I gave birth to the mother of the Lord, so that you do not err." I immediately asked, "Where then is the dear child Mary?" And she replied, "I do not have her with me now." Then I asked again, "How old is she then now?" And she replied, "Four years old." I asked her again, "Have I then just spoken with her?" And she said briefly, "Yes." I said to her, "I hope that I am not saying too much!" She did not reply and disappeared.

Now I woke up and considered all that I had seen of Mother Anne and the childhood of the holy virgin; all became clear to me and I felt very happy. When I woke up again in the morning I saw a new, very beautiful and coherent picture. I did not believe that I could forget it, but the next day so many disruptions and so much suffering came upon me that I no longer recall anything of it' (Emmerich and Brentano 1992: 72f.).

Anna Katharina Emmerick 'saw' what went on in heaven after the birth of Mary like this:

'The moment the newborn child Mary rested in the arms of her holy mother Anne, at the same time I saw it depicted in heaven before the face of the all-holy Trinity and greeted by all the heavenly hosts with indescribable joy. Then I recognized that all her bliss, pains and destiny were made known to her in a supernatural way. Mary was instructed in infinite mysteries and yet she was and remained a child. We cannot understand this knowledge of hers because our knowing has grown on the tree of knowledge. She knew all these things as a child knows its mother's breast and that it should drink from it. When the vision disappeared of how the child Mary was thus instructed by grace for heaven, I heard it weep for the first time' (ibid., 92).

Katharina saw the birth of Jesus like this:

'I saw the aura around the holy virgin become ever greater,

and the light of the lamp which Joseph had lit was no longer visible. She knelt in a wide garment without a girdle, spread round her, her face turned towards the dawn, on her rug.

In the twelfth hour of the night she was transported in prayer. I saw her raised from the earth, so that I saw the ground under her. She had her hands crossed on her breast. The aura around her increased, and everything, even inanimate things, was in joyful inner movement: the stone roof, the walls, the floor of the cave came to life in the light. Now I no longer saw the vault of the roof; a pathway of light opened above Mary to the highest heavens with increasing splendour.

In this pathway of life was a marvellous movement of glories who appeared, thronging and approaching more clearly in the form of a heavenly chorus of spirits. The holy virgin was transported in rapture and now prayed, looking down to the earth at her God whose mother she had become and who lay before her on the earth as a helpless new-born child.

I saw our Redeemer as a radiant, very small child, who outshone all the surrounding splendour with his light, lying on the mattress before the knees of the holy virgin. The child seemed to me to be very small and it grew before my eyes. But all this was only a movement of such great splendour that I cannot say with certainty how I saw it.

The holy virgin was thus enraptured for a while, and I saw how she laid a covering upon the child, but she did not take hold of it, nor did she pick it up. After some time I saw the Jesus child move and heard it weep; then it was as if Mary came to herself, and from the rug she took up the child, which she wrapped it in the covering that had been spread over it, and held it in her arms to her breast. Now she sat and covered herself and the child completely with her veil, and I believe that Mary suckled the redeemer. Then I saw around her angels in fully human form prostrating themselves in worship before the child.

It was probably an hour after the birth that Mary called St Joseph, who was still rapt in prayer . . .' (ibid., 226).

The subjective character of appearances of Mary

The visions of Anna Katharina Emmerick described above (like that of Elisabeth von Schönau) are testimonies to the blossoming fantasy of highly sensitive Catholic women and were experienced entirely on the basis of the Catholic traditions about Mary (the veneration of the mother of Mary [Anne], the resurrection and assumption of Mary). They emphatically attest how a(n imaginary) world of images can overwhelm people if *first*, certain external conditions like lack of sleep, sickness, etc. are present, and *secondly*, this religious world of images is present as a result of an institutional framework and intensive preoccupation with the object of religious veneration. That already prompts the well-founded suspicion that these visions must be said to be exclusively subjective and have nothing to do with another reality. The Mary whom the visionaries saw does not exist outside their imaginations.

Famous appearances of Mary in modern times

I shall go on to mention the most famous appearances of Mary in modern times (cf. de Rosa 1991: 354–81; Pelikan 1996: 177–87 [with bibliography]; Hanauer 1996; 1997: 85–139). These include the appearances at Lourdes (1858), Fatima in Portugal (1917) and Medjugorje in former Yugoslavia (since 1981). But they represent only a small section of the wealth of similar appearances. A book published in 1993 lists 997 appearances alone which are directly or indirectly connected with Mary, and on the Internet there is now a separate home page on appearances of Mary in the present. Here the number of appearances which have not been covered is of course an unknown factor.

Remarkably, a growth in appearances century by century

can be noted: whereas Mary showed herself only 30 times in the eighteenth century, she did so 200 times in the nineteenth century and a good 450 times in the twentieth century. Between 1930 and 1950 in Western Europe alone the church authorities investigated no less than 30 series of appearances of the mother of God and in total around 300 individual appearances, the majority of which were said to have been granted to ordinary village children. Mary felt them particularly important, calling them to prayer, penance and the rosary. It is astonishing that although all the individual recipients of visions of Mary venerated the same Lady, they often did not acknowledge one another.

'Theological' reasons for the appearances of Mary

Why does Mary think that she has to show herself increasingly often in our time? The church and theologians have said that the explanation lies in the present end-time situation. The first coming of Jesus took place in lowliness; therefore Mary also remained hidden. But the second coming of Jesus will take place in glory, and his mother is coming to prepare for this glory. This has been shown by her many appearances (thus Bishop Rudolf Graber in 1984; in Hanauer 1997: 86). It is obvious that such an understanding has no greater plausibility than the countless present-day sects which – often in contradiction to one another – read the Bible as a timetable for the last things before the return of Christ.

Empirical reasons for the visions of Mary

As is shown by the statistics given above relating to the increasing number of appearances of Mary, one can formally speak of the beginning of a tropical Marian climate both in Western Europe and in North America, of a kind that has already been observable for a long time in South America. There it began in 1531 with an appearance to the Indio Juan Diego in Guadalupe (cf. below, pp. 144f.).

In the Western world the following reasons can be given for this proneness to contagion and for the strong fascination which appearances of Mary exercise:

(a) The deep longing of believers for a personal encounter with the divine has manifestly been intensified rather than diminished both by the increasing technologizing of the world and by tendencies towards the modernization of the Catholic faith.

(b) A father God and a mother Goddess can be understood as an image of the earthly family which needs to be preserved and as a heavenly parallel to it. Only then will the world be in order again.

(c) Mary becomes the projection of ideal feminine notions of God. Moreover, as the embodiment of the loving and merciful mother she corresponds to the universal human longing for security and comes to stand beside the just father God.

(d) As a humble virgin chosen by God she serves to prompt *women* to desexualize their bodies and to be humble. At all events the plaster figure in the grotto of Lourdes virtually invites this interpretation. There one sees a Mary with downcast eyes and a body veiled to the point of being unrecognizable.

However, for reasons of depth psychology *men*, too, find pleasure in such a desexualized, pure saint. But male fantasies which style Mary a pure virgin in order to master sexual problems are unable to sublimate sexual drives in the long run. These drives discharge themselves by refunctionalizing, if not Mary herself, at least other women, as whores. Women are women and not whores or madonnas. However, some men, theologians included, never arrive at this insight.

Reasons for the official recognition of appearances of Mary

In some cases the reason for the recognition of these visions by the church is abundantly clear. Recognition as a rule takes place if the vision supports church dogmas. Thus on 11 February 1858 the fourteen-year-old Bernadette Soubirous saw in a grotto in Lourdes a 'young, wondrously beautiful lady, completely bathed in light'. Bernadette later reported that she had been 'filled with consternation' and believed that it was a 'deception'. But it was not. After interviewing her, the local bishop ordered Bernadette to ask the 'wondrously beautiful lady' her name. After being asked three times, the lady introduced herself as 'the immaculate conception'. Beyond doubt this reinforced the papal definition of this dogma which at that time was four years old, and thus at the same time furthered the official church recognition of the appearance of Mary at Lourdes. Consistently, Bernadette later said that the lady had appeared to her to confirm the pope's words. Thus this dogma received heavenly backing. The immaculate conception and papal infallibility both illustrate the same principle: the virgin could not sin; the pope could not err.

The following contemporary episode indicates how seriously Catholic dignitaries take the ghost of Mary (see Hanauer 1997: 133f.). In a sermon which Cardinal Meisner of Cologne gave in Fatima in 1990, he declared that Portugal had given room and a home there to Mary. From Fatima she had been able to begin to take Christ again to Europe and to come to the help of the oppressed disciples of her Son in the godless Communist states of Eastern Europe. To quote his words: 'I have come to thank the Portuguese for giving Mary a welcome in Fatima for this work of conversion.'

On this Josef Hanauer rightly remarks: 'Empty phrases, nothing more. Cardinal Meisner claims that Mary has brought Christ to Europe again from Fatima. Where was Christ previously? The cardinal thanks Portugal for welcoming Mary in Fatima for the work of converting Europe. One could similarly thank Yugoslavia for welcoming Mary in Medjugorje' (1997: 134). It is depressing that millions of Catholic believers take the cardinal's words as gospel truth.

Results

The examples cited here are only a fraction of the abundant appearances of Mary. In order to bring them under control – in the truest sense of the phrase – church investigating commissions have spent much time and energy examining their authenticity. For example, a number of inexplicable healings have to be demonstrated in the place concerned for church recognition to follow. Thus in Lourdes, 65 cases have been recognized by the Catholic Church as miraculous healings, whereas the doctors have designated around 1,300 cures inexplicable. The International Medical Committee of Lourdes, to which twenty-five doctors from the area of the European Union belong, meets regularly once a year to make a critical scientific examination of reports of healings in the French pilgrimage centre in the Pyrenees. In other words, the church is behaving with marked restraint towards the so-called miraculous healings.

However, I am not concerned with church approval, since in any case it has feet of clay for other reasons. For example, the Roman Church claims the authority to decide whether or not the appearances concerned are attributable to supernatural revelations brought about by God. Even a critical theologian like Karl Rahner speaks out energetically in favour of this and for example also defends the thesis that 'genuine divine prophecy is possible and has in fact occurred. Suffice it to recall Christ's prediction of the destruction of Jerusalem.' Rahner continues: 'To deny the possibility of such predictions in principle would therefore offend against the Catholic faith' (1963: 102).

Far be it from me to dispute the possibility of a revelation granted by God which could also include a prediction of the future. But critics must be allowed to test the claims to revelation: and here the reference made by Rahner to Christ's alleged prediction of the destruction of Jerusalem *fails*. All Jesus' predictions of this nature (cf. Mark 13.2; Luke 19.41–44; 21.20) were attributed to Jesus only after the

27

actual destruction of Jerusalem (cf. to this effect most recently Theissen and Merz 1998: 30). Accordingly, all the visions of Mary first need to be examined to see whether they prove to be subjective statements in the form of imagery.

At the same time it cannot be emphasized enough that visions are visual appearances of persons, things or scenes which have *no* external reality. A vision does not reach the one who receives it through the anatomical sense organs but is a product of the power of imagination or fantasy, and that applies not only to visions of Mary but also to visions of Christ.

Such distinguished critics of present-day visions of Mary as Karl Rahner and Josef Hanauer deceive themselves if they manifestly distinguish the supernatural revelation of the resurrection of Christ attested by holy scripture and church tradition from merely natural appearances and thus *a priori* boast that they have a criterion which cannot deceive. No, *all* visions have a purely subjective character. The resurrection of Jesus is grounded in seeing Jesus after his death and is accordingly to be termed a vision. It is neither without analogy nor, as a strict miracle, a revelation event brought about God – unless one knows in advance what a revelation event brought about by God is.

The real question will be how far the living reality of Jesus and his mother *interpreted* by visions has a basis in this reality. Is the basis on which Mary and Jesus are or have been understood or interpreted in the visions concerning them correct?

Mary in Protestant dogmatics and in the most recent statements from the Protestant church

Preliminary remarks

At the beginning of this chapter I showed how leading Protestant dogmatic theologians deal with the historical problems of the virgin birth. Those difficulties have become particularly evident which arise from an attempt *on the one hand* to dispute the historicity of the virgin birth and *on the other* to preserve the theological intention of the statement as binding faith. Above, I have given reasons why this can only be called a contortion.

Now given the Catholic fantasies about Mary, one could still accord a relative preference to the Protestant position. At any rate the sixteenth-century Reformers share only two of the four main mariological dogmas, and present-day Protestant dogmatic theologians are at least aware of the historical problem of the virgin birth. Nevertheless there is a striking formal parallel between Roman Catholic mariology and Protestant dogmatics, namely the rigidity in their doctrine which contains almost obsessive features (cf. Reik 1927).

The development of mariology is a general example of the way in which theological principles have been and are developed. Here castles are built in the air, each more beautiful and inviting than the next, and the whole is then regarded as the firm citadel of revealed truth. In principle, similar processes to those in mariology take place in Protestantism, for example where dogmatic theologians stubbornly insist on the sinlessness of Jesus and Jesus' disappearance from the tomb in Jerusalem as an irrefutable historical fact, or even presume to assume that according to his own witness Jesus was part of the Holy Trinity. Such assertions are just high flights of theology intent on catching the vulture who has long been circling over the structure of dogmatic thought. Protestant dogmatic theology, too, must be brought down to the ground of facts if one day it is not to suffer a crash landing – that is, if this has not already done so.

To go more deeply into this topic, at this point I shall look again at statements about Mary by Protestant theologians (cf. already above, pp. 1–4). I want to go on to report the contributions of Karl Barth and some other dogmatic theologians and, following that, to investigate the guidelines of a working party of the Evangelical Church in Germany.

Mary in Karl Barth

It is both tragic and comical that Karl Barth, the most influential theologian of the twentieth century, argued decisively for the historicity of the virgin birth – despite the results of the dispute over the Apostles' Creed in 1892. A short survey of the dispute over the Apostles' Creed, which stirred people up at the end of the nineteenth century, may illuminate this (for what follows see Lüdemann 1996: 309f.).

The dispute over the Apostles' Creed was sparked off by the dismissal of the Württemberg pastor Christoph Schrempf, who with an appeal to his conscience refused to say the Apostles' Creed at baptisms and in worship. Adolf Harnack, the most important theologian before the First World War, was asked for his opinion on the Schrempf affair by students in Berlin and gave an answer at the end of the summer semester of 1892; it was published the same year. It raised a storm of protest and provoked declarations of solidarity, but in the end they all ran into the sand – as did Harnack's own opinion. Strange though it may seem, the dispute over the Apostles' Creed tended further to reinforce the juxtaposition of academic theology and practical work, with no link between them. Whereas this controversy was originally about the honesty of pastors in office, the whole affair was trivialized by the academic discussion. For one can have an endless academic discussion about the significance of the Apostles' Creed without changing the distress of the pastor in the slightest. In the end, fruitless academic disputes took the place of the overdue reform of worship. The same thing is happening today, where almost anything can be said in church and theology without there being any chance of changing liturgy and the shape of worship.

A regression began with Karl Barth which had the advantage of at least bridging the gulf between the pastorate and academic theology. Although as a pupil of Adolf Harnack Karl Barth *must have* known that the virgin birth was

historically false, he resolutely spoke our for its historicity –
one must probably say, against his conscience.

In the 1927 *Christian Dogmatics in Outline*, Barth
connects the virgin birth closely with the resurrection of
Jesus:

'That Christ rises from the dead is grounded in it and is
therefore unavoidably to be taught because he is the one
who was miraculously conceived and born. That he is the
one who was miraculously conceived and born discloses
itself, shows itself, makes itself known, in his resurrection.
Only miracle is the basis for miracle, and only through
miracle can miracle be recognized. Thus there is no
evasion, no misunderstanding, no ambivalence about the
"*Deus dixit*" [= God has spoken, GL] which is the issue
here' (1927: 275).

However, in his view the person of the virgin Mary could
not be the subject of any independent dogmatic interest. For
she is made mother of God solely by God alone: 'It is not her
virginity that is the miracle of revelation and reconciliation
but God's act in her, the virgin, and that is twofold' (281).

The *Church Dogmatics* develops these thoughts further,
but does not introduce anything essentially new (a) with
reference to the historicity of the virgin birth and (b) with
reference to the role of Mary.

(a) The 'born of the Virgin Mary' is now no longer seen
intrinsically as a parallel to the resurrection, but as a parallel
to the empty tomb (1956: 183). Both the virgin birth and the
empty tomb did not represent *conditions* for the new beginning that took place in Jesus Christ or for his resurrection but
signs of them. But we cannot have the substance without the
sign: no one could say that the empty tomb in itself had the
power 'to unveil for the disciples the veiled fact that "God
was in Christ". But was it revealed to them otherwise than by
the sign of this external fact?' (179). The same is true of the
virgin birth: 'May it not be the case that the only one who

hears the witness of the things is the one who keeps to the sign by which the witness has actually signified it?' (180).

So it is not surprising that Barth's answer to the 'question of popular theology, whether in order to believe in a really Christian way "one" would have to believe fully in the virgin birth', is: 'there is certainly nothing to prevent anyone, without affirming the doctrine of the Virgin birth, from recognizing the mystery of the person of Jesus or from believing in a perfectly Christian way. It is within God's counsel and will to make this possible.' But this does not imply that the church is at liberty to convert the doctrine of the virgin birth into an option for specially strong or for specially weak souls. 'If the servants of the church should include some who doubt the Virgin birth, they are to be required to treat their private road as a private road and . . . not make it an object of their proclamation . . . If they personally cannot affirm it and so (unfortunately) withhold it from their congregations, they must at least pay the dogma the respect of keeping silence about it' (181)

It is only a short step to see these schizophrenic remarks of Barth as in fact an insidious invitation to hypocrisy. Here, to paraphrase Adolf Harnack freely, the nonsense and authority of revelation seem to some degree to be the stamp of higher truth.

(b) The significance of the Virgin Mary is exhausted in the 'through grace alone' that she represents. 'In the form of non-willing, non-achieving, non-creative, non-sovereign man who can merely receive, merely be ready, merely let something be done to and with himself', she has nothing of her own to offer the God who acts (191). Her virginity does not form, say, the starting point for the divine grace. Mary is not God's fellow-worker, has no control (192). At this point no door opens which could lead to mariology (195).

According to Barth, the designation of Mary as 'mother of God' does not contradict this:

'To a certain extent it amounts to a test of the proper

32

understanding of the incarnation of the Word, that as Christians and theologians we do not reject the description of Mary as "the mother of God", but in spite of its being overloaded by the so-called Mariology of the Roman Catholic Church, we affirm and approve of it as a legitimate expression of christological truth. We must not omit to defend it against the misuse made of the knowledge expressed in this description. But the knowledge in question and so the description as well must not for that reason be suppressed' (1956: 138).

In his 1947 *Dogmatics in Outline*, Barth sums up his view of the historicity of the virgin birth as follows:

'The miracle of Christmas is the actual form of the mystery of the personal union of God and man ... Again and again the Christian Church and its theology has insisted that we cannot postulate that the reality of the Incarnation, the mystery of Christmas, had by absolute necessity to take the form of this miracle. The true Godhead and the true humanity of Jesus Christ in their unity do not depend on the fact that Christ was conceived by the Holy Spirit and born of the Virgin Mary. All that we can say is that it pleased God to let the mystery be real and become manifest in this shape and form. But again that cannot mean that over against this factual form of the miracle we are as it were free to affirm it or not to affirm it, to make a deduction and say that we have listened, but make a reservation, that this matter could be also in another form for us. We perhaps best understand the relation of matter and form, which is presented here, by taking a look at the story ... of the healing of the paralytic (Mark 2.10): "That you may know that the Son of Man has power to forgive sins.. . Arise, take up your bed and go your way." "That you may know . . ."; in this way the miracle of the Virgin Birth is also to be understood' (1949: 100).

Conclusion: however much Barth's repudiation of any kind of mariology runs counter to Roman Catholic doctrine, one may still encounter his inexorable insistence on the historicity of the virgin birth. Anyone who thus decrees so sharply 'from above' and thinks that he can scotch the doubts of serious searchers by condemning them to silence already knows that the virgin birth is a historical event before he has asked himself about the historical problem that it really poses. The impression is forced home that here someone has recognized that to yield on this one point would make the whole ramshackle wall of dogmatics totter.

However, the gentle objection that Wolf Krötke thinks that he has to make to Barth's view of the virgin birth only barely touches on the matter. For in doubting that 'the late witnesses to the virgin birth have the same significance as the stories about the tomb in connection with the testimony to the resurrection event' (1996: 14), he is evidently unaware that it does not make sense to weigh the significance of these two equally unhistorical events against each other.

Further Protestant statements on the virgin birth

Wolfgang Trillhaas certainly concedes that we cannot speak unthinkingly about the virgin birth 'either as a "historical fact" or as a "saving fact"'. But what the statement about the virgin birth *means* is 'an indispensable concern of Christian faith with Jesus Christ'.

> 'Jesus is not a saviour who is born, not someone who becomes a saviour. Jesus does not stand in the old complex of human sin and guilt, but is a new man, a new beginning. The event of Jesus Christ is not from human beings; it is from God' (1972: 265).

The miracle of the incarnation of Jesus Christ is not tied to the physical virginity of Mary, since God can 'perform his miracles even in the hiddenness of the natural context' (ibid.).

Jürgen Moltmann states that it is a total misunderstanding of its nature 'to call the virgin birth "historical", let alone "biological"' (1990, 82).

> 'Modern positivist characterizations of this kind do anything but preserve the intention and truth of the story. In actual fact they destroy it. The narrators' aim is not to report a gynaecological miracle. Their aim is to confess Jesus as the messianic Son of God and to point at the very beginning of his life to the divine origin of his person' (ibid.).

Furthermore, theologians of the early church saw the virgin birth less as a sign of the divinity of Christ than as a sign of his true humanity, in opposition to Gnostic tendencies: 'If we wished to bring out this intention of the nativity story today, we should have to stress the non-virginal character of Christ's birth' (84). For this reason Moltmann argues for speaking of a birth of Christ 'from the Spirit' instead of a virgin birth (87).

Moreover the understanding of the significance of Mary is corrected in the light of this: 'If we take the birth of Christ from the Spirit seriously, then much that the church has ascribed to "the Virgin Mary" is transposed to God the Holy Spirit himself, and Mary can once again be that which she was and is: the Jewish mother of Jesus' (86).

One cannot protest energetically enough against Moltmann that according to him the New Testament texts evidently no longer mean why they explicitly say. When Moltmann says at another point, referring to the feminine gender of the Hebrew word *ruach* (= spirit), 'God is the father of Jesus Christ and therefore the Holy Spirit is his divine mother. Therefore mariology is not a question of gynaecology, but a topic of Christian pneumatology' (1988: 22), the question immediately arises whether Jesus – according to Matthew and Luke – was fathered by a woman. Here the over-hasty modernization of biblical texts takes its revenge.

The 'ecumenical dogmatics' of Edmund Schlink again brings out the similarity between resurrection and virgin birth – the 'process of procreation through the Holy Spirit remains hidden in the same way as does the resurrection' (1983, 284) – and maintains the historicity of the virgin birth. Its historicity, like that of the resurrection of Jesus, can be repudiated only where the principle of analogy, i.e. the principle that historical process are in principle all of the same kind, is used 'dogmatically' (ibid., 285). I would be interested to know whether Schlink would deal as generously with all other texts from antiquity which similarly predicate the virgin birth of sons of God (cf. below, pp. 72–6).

For further examples of similarly unsatisfactory expedients adopted by Protestant dogmatic theologians over the virgin birth cf. already above, pp. 1–4.

A new Protestant contribution on Mary. The most recent developments

In 1988 the Catholica working party of the United Evangelical Lutheran Church of Germany approved some guidelines, 'Mary, the Mother of the Lord'. These were also published three years later as a book (= Kiessig 1991), enlarged by some Orthodox, Roman Catholic, Protestant and feminist contributions. This can be regarded as a semi-official statement of the Evangelical Church in Germany, and is meant to 'clarify and deepen personal faith' and help towards 'dialogue with Roman Catholic Christians' (1991: 8). To this end biblical texts in which Mary plays a role are collected, together with pictures, verses of hymns, prayers, liturgical passages, quotations from Luther and brief reflections.

The concern of the authors to expound all the statements about Mary in terms of Christ and subordinate them to him is manifest. For example, they say that the title 'Mother of God' means 'that Mary is the mother of the one who as true man is also true God and has revealed God's nature and will in a unique, clear and final way' (16). Mary has no significance of her own for faith. 'She is only a wonderful example of the working of God in human beings. Christians who have no personal relationship to Mary therefore lack nothing necessary for their faith' (18).

Thus far there is a clear distancing from Roman Catholic mariology here. Nevertheless there are unmistakable concessions to the Roman Catholic side. For example it remains unclear how far the statements cited above are compatible with the statement that as mother of the Redeemer, Mary 'has a particularly important place in the history of salvation and thus in the communion of saints' (82). The reassuring statement that whether theological statements about the conception of Jesus by the Holy Spirit and the virgin birth are 'to be understood only metaphorically or at the same time historically and biologically is a question over which the views of Christians can differ' (14) is also strange. Has historical criticism been working in vain here for two hundred and fifty years?

The conclusion of the guidelines is: 'Thus Mary also has her place in the life of faith of the Evangelical Lutheran Church and to discover this can be a task which strengthens the faith of Protestant Christians' (88).

The use of scripture in the guidelines can only be described as pre-critical. Here are just a few examples from an abundance of exegetical monstrosities:

(a) That the New Testament contains various views of Jesus' origin, some of which are opposed to one another, is concealed. Thus for example a quotation from a hymn in which Jesus is described as 'the virgin's son' is followed by the assertion that the apostle Paul says 'the same thing in different words' and a quotation of Gal. 4.4–7 (37). In reality this text, like all Paul's other statements about the origin of Jesus, is hardly compatible with talk of the virgin birth. Rather, the apostle puts forward a christology of pre-existence and incarnation which shows no interest in the virgin birth.

37

(b) In connection with the Christmas story in Luke the guidelines say that here 'what the prophet Isaiah had announced many centuries before is fulfilled in a miraculous form, surpassing all intimations' (36). The fact that Isa.7.14 does not speak of a virgin but of a 'young woman' is suppressed, as is the fact that the context of the scene in Isa.7.10ff., which is in any case fictitious, beyond doubt calls for an event which takes place while king Ahaz is still alive (he died in 725 BCE) (cf. Lüdemann 1997: 8–12).

(c) The authors quote a statement by Ulrich Wilckens that with her Magnificat (= Luke 1.46–55) Mary stands 'in the series of Old Testament prophets' who 'with incorruptible harshness and clarity proclaim the imminent judgment of God on all human arrogance in the political and social sphere' (13). The fact that Mary never spoke the Magnificat is not mentioned.

(d) In view of this it is hardly surprising that one does not hear anything about the legendary character of the infancy narratives in Matthew and Luke either. However, the authors of the guidelines are not at all afraid of harmonizing the mutually contradictory narratives in Matthew and Luke. In their remarks on Matt. 2.1–12 they say that the astronomers from the East offered 'the child their gifts without being offended that the manger in Bethlehem is not at all fitting for a new-born king' (42). Since previously it was emphasized that the astronomers were not kings, one has to suppose that the authors did not want to ask to much of popular piety after this harsh blow. So what does it matter that there is not a word about a manger in the Gospel of Matthew?

These guidelines, in which key representatives of German Protestantism, including Ulrich Wilckens, former professor of New Testament and later bishop of the North Elbe church, have been involved, thus clearly have considerable defects and encourage ignorance among Protestant church members, especially also about the person of the 'virgin' Mary. For – and this cannot be emphasized often enough – these church members are constantly subjected to the influence of worship and its liturgy, which can only be broken by decisive measures and relentless enlightenment, even if strong efforts at restoration are widespread in times of financial difficulties like the present. In my view these efforts are so strenuous that today it would presumably be no longer possible to implement the ordination of women in German Protestantism.

It is probably no chance that in the new top Protestant encyclopaedia, the *Theologische Realenzyklopädie* (*TRE*), the word 'Mary/Marian piety' is dealt with quite comprehensively (Vol.22, 1992, 115–61; cf. by comparison the brief article in the third edition of *Die Religion in Geschichte und Gegenwart* [*RGG*], Vol.IV, 763–70). But Mary is also increasingly playing an important role in current theological trends, like feminist theology and liberation theology. Therefore it is time once again to bring out what we can know about Mary in a generally understandably way. Here my simple presupposition is that historical knowledge must be the basis of theological judgments. Anything else leads to an easygoing position which may boast that it respects the (superstitious) traditions of others but threatens to sink into randomness. I found this most recently in reading the latest book about Mary (Gaventa 1995). Right at the beginning, the author excuses herself for not having discussed the question of the virginity of Mary *after* the birth of Jesus as well, and defends herself against the suspicion of wanting to devalue the tradition of others (IX). May one no longer say, for example, that the tradition of the perpetual virginity of Mary was historical nonsense?

2

Mary in the New Testament and in the Christian Sources outside the New Testament: Redaction, Tradition, History

The procedure

The following writings of the New Testament speak directly or indirectly of the mother of Jesus:

- the letters of the apostle Paul to the Galatians (c. 51 CE) and to the Romans (c. 53 CE);
- the earliest Gospel (Mark), from around 70; early second-century tradition attributed it to Mark, the so-called interpreter of the apostle Peter;
- the first Gospel (Matt.) – later attributed to the disciple Matthew – , which was composed, presumably in Antioch, around 90 CE, using Mark and other special sources and the Sayings source which it has in common with Luke;
- the Gospel of Luke and the Acts of the Apostles; only in the second century did collectors in the church associate these two writings, addressed around the end of the first century to a certain Theophilus, with Paul's companion, Luke;
- the Fourth Gospel (John), which in the appendix (ch.21) is attributed to the Beloved Disciple (John 21.23f.), whom church circles in the middle of the second century wrongly identified with John the son of Zebedee. The final form of

the Fourth Gospel, which has been worked over several times, comes from the beginning of the second century.

The last book of the Bible, the Revelation of John, does not contain any reference to Mary, since the woman from Rev.12, who bore a son and fled into the wilderness (Rev.12.5f.), has nothing to do with Mary but refers to Israel, from whom the Messiah comes.

Presumably old tradition appears in the following witnesses outside the New Testament:

- in the Gospel of Thomas, a collection of 114 logia of Jesus from the beginning of the second century, found in 1945;
- in the Protevangelium of James, a work from the end of the second century composed to glorify Mary, which above all reflects the Jewish-Christian controversy over the birth of Jesus from Mary;
- in the work of the Platonic philosopher Celsus, who in the second half of the second century wrote the first polemical work against the young church under the title 'True Word' and in it hands on Jewish criticism of Mary.

The so-called Acts of Pilate from the middle of the second century, which on the basis of the New Testament Gospels offer romance-like descriptions, among other things, of the trial of Jesus, are certainly important evidence for the ongoing development of New Testament traditions; however, they are not relevant to a historical investigation of the real circumstances of the birth of Jesus, as their statements about this (2.2–6) presuppose the Gospel of Matthew and do not contain any earlier tradition.

The same thing applies where, for example, Jewish Christians in the second century use Matthew without the prehistory (chs.1 and 2) and suppose that Jesus was indeed the Messiah, but born as a human being with human parents (cf. Justin, *Dial.*48,4). The paternity of Joseph implied here does not go back to the very earliest time but is a recessive development on the basis of Matthew. Therefore I shall not discuss these and similar texts further here. For example, no one would think of dating Gnostic teachings about Joseph as the natural father of Jesus back to the earliest period. Cf. e.g. Gospel of Philip 91: 'Philip the apostle said: "Joseph the carpenter planted a garden because he needed wood for his trade. It was he who made the cross from the trees which he planted. And (so) his seed hung on that which he planted. His seed was Jesus, but the planting was the cross." ' Here, too, individual passages of the New Testament will have been the occasion for such statements. They can therefore be left out of account in the framework of this work (cf. the rich survey in Campenhausen 1979: 80–5, with a different assessment).

I shall go through the texts in their generally accepted chronological order, each time in three stages. The *first* stage discusses what the final author means to say ('Redaction'); here, depending on the nature of the text, I may begin with remarks about the origin and nature of the text and the way in which it is constructed. The *second* stage is concerned with the tradition on which the final author may be presumed to have worked ('Tradition'). The *third* stage defines the historical value of the tradition ('History'). In the translation of the texts which precedes each discussion the source-critical result of the following analysis is already taken into account in that – as far as possible – redactional constructions and additions by the final author are in each case distinguished from the traditions available to him by being printed in italics.

The *advantage* of such a procedure is that the character of each individual writing is taken seriously and it is not just exploited as a source of information about what is reported in it. The latter course is not possible, above all because none of the authors of the documents investigated here was an eye-witness. Thus the character of the early Christian writings about Mary also requires the method chosen here, which has proved itself a thousand times in the analysis of New Testament texts on other topics.

The *disadvantage* of this approach is that it does not initially take into account the general knowledge of the individual authors which may possibly be hidden in the redactional work. Thus the charge of reductionism can always be made against the course adopted here, even if in my view there is no other method which promises success. However, I shall take account of this objection in the analysis, as far as the text allows it.

Paul

Gal. 4.4
The birth of the son of God from a woman

'But when the time was fulfilled, God sent his Son, born of a woman and born under the law.'

Redaction

This verse is embedded in a section about liberation from the law through Christ. For a certain period the Galatians had been in 'slavery to the powers of the world' (v.3) and accordingly had observed 'specific days, months and times and years' (v.10). But now God had sent his son in order to redeem those who were under the law, namely under the powers of the world, and opened up the possibility of their becoming children. In the immediate context of the passage quoted, Paul describes the state of childhood like this: 'And because you are now children, God has sent the spirit of his son into our hearts, crying "Abba, dear Father!" So you are no longer a slave but a child; and if a child, then also an heir through God' (Gal. 4.6f.).

Within the framework of this act of redemption, God causes Jesus to be born of a woman whose name Paul does not give; the choice of the word 'woman' (Greek *gyne*) does not in itself indicate whether Paul envisages a married or an unmarried women. (Had he been asked, though, the apostle would doubtless have opted for a married woman, since he regarded sexual intercourse outside marriage as fornication; cf. I Cor.7.2: 'But because of [the danger of] fornication, each man should have his own wife and each woman her own husband.') Through his birth Jesus was put under the law. For Paul, Jesus' mother thus belongs to the time that is past. But the son of God was sent in order to redeem those who were under the law and thus to form the basis of a new relationship between God and human beings.

Mary as a person has no theological role in this passage. Nor is she specifically mentioned in any other passage in the letters of Paul.

Tradition

Either Paul was given the information that Jesus was born of a woman or he inferred it himself. At all events the starting point for this report is the belief that God has sent his son and caused him to become a human being. The sending does not necessarily presuppose that the person concerned is born of a virgin. For example, John the Baptist was also sent by God (cf. John 1.6), and no one thought that he had been born of a virgin.

History

It is impossible to answer the historical question which immediately arises, whether Paul knew the name of Jesus' mother and whether he also knew of the virgin birth. Paul knew more than he wrote in his letters, and wrote more letters than those which have been preserved. But it is significant that he made relatively many different statements about Jesus, and none of them even hints at birth from a virgin.

Rom. 1.3–4
The fleshly descent and the appointment of the son of God

'. . . (God's son), who was descended from David *according to the flesh* and was appointed son of God in power *according to the Spirit* of holiness through/since the resurrection of the dead.'

Redaction

The verses quoted are part of the prescript of the letter to the Romans in which the apostle, who is sending it, introduces himself to the community in Rome, which is unknown to him. He says that he has been called to be an apostle of Jesus Christ, set apart for the gospel of God (Rom.1.1–2). This accords with other statements that Paul makes about himself. According to him, the son of God was revealed to him so that he might preach the gospel to the Gentiles (cf. Gal. 1.15f.). According to Rom.1.3 Jesus is already son of God during his earthly existence and was already son of God before he became man. Paul is at one with the Roman Christians in believing in him. The additions 'according to the flesh' in v.3 and 'according to the spirit' in v.4 indicate that for Paul the earthly Jesus counts only in the light of the risen son of God.

Tradition

For a long time it has been established that a tradition is being used in vv.3–4. This is indicated first by the un-Pauline language; secondly by the formal participial style (which is possible only in Greek); and thirdly by the un-Pauline content of individual statements. Thus according to the tradition Jesus was first appointed son of God since or through the resurrection of the dead, whereas for Paul he was already son of God on entering into human existence (cf. the text Gal. 4.4 analysed on pp. 43f. above). The supposed text of the

45

formula runs, 'Descended from David, appointed son of God in power through/since the resurrection of the dead.'

History

The tradition does not contain any kind of reference to the miraculous birth of Jesus. Rather, he is a descendant of the family of David, a Davidide. Whether this claim was made through his mother or through his father is not said.

So this second text of Paul's, too, contributes nothing to our investigation of the son of the virgin and his mother, although of course it presupposes the birth of Jesus from a woman.

The Gospel of Mark

Mark 3.20–35:
The relatives and the true kinsfolk of Jesus

Redaction

In chapter 3 the earliest Gospel contains a fundamental statement about the relationship of Jesus to his mother and vice versa. It appears within a section (Mark 3.20–35) which displays Mark's typical technique of interlocking. Compare the large number of instances – each time the encapsulated narrative is put in brackets: 5.21–43 (vv.25–34); 6.7–30 (vv.14–29); 11.12–25 (vv.15–19); 14.1–11 (vv.3–9); 14.54–72 (vv.55–65). The other New Testament Gospels which use Mark quite often eliminate the interlocking, which is one more reason for regarding it as part of Mark's style. As usual, here he has broken up a consecutive tradition and has incorporated a further narrative into it for greater dramatic effect.

Mark 3.20–31 run:

'20 And he (Jesus) went into a house. And the crowd came

together again, so that they could not even eat. 21 And when his own heard it, they went out to seize him, for they said, "He is out of his mind." '

In this passage, on grounds of language and content, v.20 derives wholly from Mark, but v.21 forms the beginning of the piece of tradition which Mark has torn apart.

After this, a story about 'Jesus and the evil spirits' has been encapsulated (vv.22–30), in which scribes from Jerusalem accuse Jesus of being possessed (v.22). This attack escalates the charge of Jesus' kinsfolk made in v.21 and is put by Mark in the mouth of the scribes. For Mark, Jerusalem is the hostile city in which Jesus will be killed and which is therefore doomed to destruction. For him, scribes from Jerusalem are thus the worst possible opponents.

Then (Mark 3.31–35) the story begun in vv.20–21 continues:

'31 And his mother and his brothers came; and standing outside they sent to him and had him called. 32 *And the people were sitting about him.* And they said to him, "Your mother and your brothers are outside, asking for you." 33 And he replied, "Who are my mother and my brothers?" 34 And looking around on those who sat about him, he said "Here are my mother and my brothers. 35 Whoever does the will of God is my brother, and sister, and mother." '

[31–33] Mark further describes 'his own' from v.20 as the physical family of Jesus. Jesus redefines his family after a question from the people (v.32).
[34–35] Only those who do the will of God can be Jesus' brothers, sisters or mother. Here the absence of Jesus' father is striking. Mark 10.29–30 provides the key to understanding this passage: 'Jesus said, "Truly, I say to you, there is no one who has left house or brothers or sisters or mother or father or children or fields, for my sake and for the gospel, who

47

will not receive a hundredfold now in this time, houses and brothers and sisters and mothers and children and fields, and in the age to come eternal life."' Both passages reflect a community of Jesus' disciples which knows no father of a Roman patriarchal kind. That need not contradict the theological foundation that according to Jesus all have the same heavenly father and therefore need no earthly father.

Tradition

Mark had before him a tradition which formed the basis of vv.21, 31–35. It can be described as an ideal scene in which Jesus speaks about his true family.

History

Two nuclei of tradition are contained in the ideal scene which suggest historical bedrock:

(a) Jesus' family thinks him crazy (v.21). Such a report would be too offensive to have been invented. Moreover, in their use of Mark, Matthew and Luke omit this detail and provide no substitute (see pp. 88f. and 125 below). In other words, they *delete* it.

(v) Verse 35 reflects the social structure of communities of the followers of Jesus before and/or after 'Easter' (cf. above on the redaction). The verse reflects the situation of settled converts who had been rejected by their families (cf. Luke 14.26/Matt. 10.37) and promises them a substitute social family. It would be attractive to locate this situation in the Jesus movement, even if there are strong reasons for assuming a later phase.

Accordingly, v.35 contributes nothing to the question whether Jesus had brothers and sisters, and there is the additional problem whether these could be translated as cousins.

Mark 6.1–6
The rejection of Jesus, the son of Mary, in his ancestral city

'1. *He went away from there.* And he came into his ancestral city; *and his disciples followed him.* 2 And on the sabbath *he began to teach in the synagogue*; and many heard him and were astonished, saying, "Where did this man get all this? What is the wisdom given to him? *What miracles are wrought by his hands?* 3 Is not this *the craftsman*, the son of Mary *and brother of James and Joses and Judas and Simon, and are not his sisters here with us?"* And they took offence at him.
4 And Jesus said to them, "A prophet is not without honour, except in his ancestral city, *and among his kin, and in his house."*
5 *And he could do no miracle there, except that he laid his hands upon a few sick people and healed them. 6 And he marvelled at their unbelief. And he went about among the villages teaching.'*

Redaction

[1a] This transition, and the mention in v.1b of the disciples, who have no role in what follows, derive from Mark.
[2a] This contains the typically Markan motif of Jesus teaching and thus recalls Jesus' appearance in Capernaum (1.21–28); cf. esp. 1.21f.: '21 And they went into Capernaum; and immediately on the sabbath he entered the synagogue and taught. 22 And they were astonished at his teaching, for he taught them as one who had authority, and not as the scribes.' Because of the frequent occurrence of the miracle motif (cf. v.5) and the miracles in the context (ch.5 alone contains three massive miracles), the question about Jesus' miracles in v.2b may similarly be redactional.
[3] The audience's question brings out the fact that there is nothing unusual about Jesus: after all, he is the craftsman

49

they all know. Similarly, his brothers and sisters are known. *Therefore* offence is taken at his special claim (for the unusual phrase 'son of Mary' instead of 'son of Joseph' cf. the analysis of the tradition).

[4] The second half derives from the redactional link between wisdom maxim and narrative.

[5] The miracle motif is redactional (see above on v.2).

[6] With the closing remark in v.6a, the word-group belief/unbelief appears for the fourth time within the major section 4.31–6.6a, and is therefore the bracket which holds it together. Because of their belief people expect miracles of Jesus; indeed, like the woman with an issue of blood (5.25–34) they can make Jesus involuntarily perform a miracle. So in this section Mark is encouraging his readers to believe that Jesus performs miracles. The scene and the behaviour of people in his ancestral city are the negative counterpart to this.

Tradition

Possibility 1: Mark 6.1–6 provides a model example of the way in which a narrative has been formed out of a wisdom maxim (v.4a). The link word prompting the composition of the story is 'ancestral city' (vv.1, 4).

Possibility 2: verse 4a, the wisdom maxim, has been inserted by Mark into a story of the unsuccessful appearance of Jesus in his home town. Mark has been stimulated by the key word 'ancestral city' to add the wisdom maxim. This possibility is more probable: the maxim in v.4a is an attempt to explain the fact of Jesus' lack of success, which is hard to understand and offensive to the Christian community.

The form of the story of Jesus' unsuccessful appearance in his home town can no longer be determined with certainty. It may be general knowledge which Mark had.

In the tradition, the comment that Jesus is the son of Mary stands out as an argument against him. Mark evidently tones down this argument by a neutral family catalogue, which because of the names given in it may go back to tradition. But the phrase 'son of Mary' remains all the more unusual since a Jewish male would normally be associated with the name of his father (but cf. the study by Ilan 1992), even if his father was already dead (against Brown et al. 1978: 64; cf. also Ilan 1992: 23 n.3 for inscriptional evidence). Compare the names of some well-known rabbinic teachers: Johanan ben Zakkai, Akiba ben Joseph, Hananiah ben Dosa.

There are some exceptions to this rule in the Old Testament.

(a) Naming after the mother occurs regularly where the sons come from one father but different mothers; cf. Gen. 21.9: son of Hagar as opposed to son of Sarah, etc.

A further example confirms this: Solomon wants to dispute the right of Adonijah the son of Haggith (I Kings 1.5, 11; 2.13) to the throne. Both are sons of David, but Adonijah is introduced as the son of Haggith because Solomon is the son of Bathsheba. Without this situation of rivalry, both would be called sons of David.

(b) At some points in the Old Testament there may be remnants of matriarchal thinking, for example when in II Sam. 2.18 etc. three of David's military leaders are named after their mothers (the sons of Zeruiah: Joab, Asahel and Abishai).

(c) Naming after the mother takes place in mixed marriages between Gentiles and a Jewish woman (cf. Lev. 24.10f.: son of Shelomith).

(d) However, naming after the mother does not take place if the father is dead: I Kings 17.17 does not tell against this, since the naming after the mother is governed by the fact that the father is a Gentile. Luke 7.12 (the only son of his mother') does not tell against it either, since this remark is governed by the fact that the woman, a widow, had been dependent on her son's help.

(e) Illegitimate sons were not named after their father but after their mother: Jephthah, son of a harlot (Judg. 11.1).

Perhaps David's designation of himself as son of Ruth also belongs here (cf. Neusner 1993: 103–9). This self-designation stands in the context of the charge that David was descended from Ruth the Moabite, who was born a Gentile. Cf. Midrash Ruth on Ruth 4.18: (David:) 'How long will they be agitated about me and say, "Does not his family have a blemish (to marry into Israel)? Is he not descended from the Moabite woman Ruth?"' David defends himself against this by pointing out to his Jewish enemies that they themselves have a blemish and are descended from two sisters, Leah and Rachel, to whom Jacob would not have been allowed to be married at the same time (cf. Lev. 18.18).

The discussion about David as son of Ruth illuminates the background of the polemic against Jesus as son of Mary. In David's case, too, the issue was illegitimacy in the broader sense. The common feature – we can say in advance – is *not* the shared pagan descent of both mothers (thus, however, Seeberg 1918 and Hirsch 1939) or grandmothers, since Mary is a Jewish woman. Her Jewish name Mary = Miriam already suggests this. However, illegitimacy may well have been an issue; otherwise Jesus would not have been named after his mother.

Over against this it is sometimes conjectured that the designation 'son of Mary' is based on a veneration of Mary as mother of the Lord which was possibly already beginning – here the mere fact of her motherhood would be sufficient explanation (thus Gnilka 1989: 231f.). However, that is improbable (see below).

In addition, it has been argued that the identification of Jesus by his mother may simply imply that Mary had a higher social status (Ilan 1992: 44). Apart from the lack of sources to support such a thesis, this fails to account for the difficulties which early Christians had with the expression 'son of Mary'.

At all events the expression 'son of Mary' comes from a tradition which was current in the very first period, soon stamped by controversy over the authority of Jesus.

The two parallel passages, in Matthew and Luke, each of which change 'son of Mary' into 'son of Joseph' or 'son of the craftsman', provide a substantial reason for assuming that 'son of Mary' is meant *polemically*. Moreover reference should be made to the textual tradition of Mark: a Gospel papyrus from the third century (slightly damaged at this point) with a probability bordering on certainty makes the following correction to the text: 'Is this not the son of the craftsman and Mary?' (Papyrus 45).

At the end of this analysis of the tradition, here once again are the three most important reasons for assuming that the phrase 'son of Mary' focusses on Jesus' lack of legitimacy:

1. The phrase is used in Jesus' home town, which was either Nazareth or Capernaum. Note that the name Nazareth is not part of the tradition behind Mark 6, but is only added by Luke (4.16) in his reworking of Mark 6.1–6 on the basis of Mark 1.9. On the other hand, according to Matthew Capernaum is the actual residence of Jesus (Matt. 8–9 with the comments by Strecker 1971: 93–8).

2. It appears on the lips of those who have not fully understood Jesus or are hostile to him.

3. Mark does not repeat the statement in Mark 6.3. He does not answer the charge by rejecting it, but by declaring the kinsfolk unimportant in v.4b.

In conclusion it may also be asked whether the charge of being without honour in Mark 6.4a is not directly connected with the contemptuous phrase 'son of Mary'. Compare Wisdom 3.16f.: '16 But children of adulterers will not come to maturity, and the offspring of an unlawful union will perish. 17 Even if they live long they will be held of no account, and finally their old age will be *without honour* . . .'

That would mean that Jesus was without honour because he was of illegitimate descent.

With its second part detached, the saying underlying Mark 6.4 perhaps goes back to Jesus. But it could also have been put on the lips of Jesus later.

Historically, we can discover that the designation of Jesus as 'son of Mary' was already used against him in his home town. In that case the phrase is to be described as a taunt term which points the finger at a weak point in Jesus' genealogy. For the agitated people of his home town to call their fellow-countryman Jesus son of Mary is a bitter insult. The key to understanding it is that Jesus is contemptuously called after his mother and not after his father, as was customary. So what the charge is saying is: this boy who wants to preach at us does not have a proper father; he is a bastard (cf. Stauffer 1969).

If this historical reconstruction is correct, another aspect of Mark's understanding of the scene emerges: he tones down the mockery by inserting it into a neutral family catalogue. Accordingly, one possible objection to the interpretation above, that an accusation of descent outside marriage (v.3) would have called for an answer from Jesus, disappears. Note in addition that the brothers and sisters of Jesus are not also named after their mother Mary.

The following three understandings of the text are off the mark:

(a) Mark removed the name Joseph from the tradition behind Mark 6.3 because Joseph had no place of honour in the Jerusalem church. At the same time this amounted to a manifesto against the legal and doctrinal hegemony of the Jerusalem church. Hence the positive lack of interest in Joseph. This is a second-degree hypothesis.

(b) The statement that Jesus is the son of Mary is an indirect reference to the virgin birth. For otherwise we would expect Jesus to have been called Joseph's son. But that cannot be read out of the text, all the less so since at no point does Mark show interest in the virgin birth.

(c) In his important article on the question of the origin of Jesus, McArthur thinks that the term 'son of Mary' is related to the situation: 'Oh yes! That's Mary's boy from down the street' (1973: 57). But what would be the point of this informal expression in such a dramatic scene (cf. rightly Brown et al. 1978: 61 n.108)?

Once again, at this point the father of Jesus is not named because there is no doubt about who his real father is. Had Jesus been a physical son of Joseph the expression 'son of Mary' would never have found its way into an early Christian text. The phrase 'son of Mary' is so shocking that only Mark has the courage to repeat it.

The anti-Christian Jewish traditions about the birth of Jesus

The question now arises as to whether the hypothesis developed in the analysis of the texts in Mark can be supported by Jewish sources which stand close to it in time.

The *Toledoth Jeshu,* a collection of popular romances about Jesus, report the seduction of the young Mary in detail (cf. Krauss 1902: Schlichting 1982). However, they can be ruled out on chronological grounds, since they come from the Middle Ages. The rabbinic sources of the Tannaitic period (up to 220 CE) can equally be ruled out, since at no point do they mention Mary and Jesus (cf. Maier 1978: 268).

These sobering judgments do not mean that there was no Jewish polemic against the church at this point in the second century. However, it is difficult to identify.

There is clear Jewish criticism (a) in a church father from the middle of the second century and (b) in the earliest extant pagan writing against the Christians, a generation later.

(a) Justin Martyr

In his dialogue with the Jew Trypho (= *Dial*), Justin (died 162 CE) twice comes to speak of Jewish charges against Jesus. In

Dial. 69.7 he mentions that Jesus is regarded as a magician and one who leads the people astray. *Dial.*108.2 takes up the assertion of *Dial.*17.1 about Palestine emissaries to the Diaspora and gives the following warning to the Jewish Diaspora communities:

> 'Yet you not only have not repented, after you learned that he rose from the dead, but you have sent . . . chosen and ordained men throughout all the world to proclaim that a godless and lawless sect *(hairesis)* had sprung from a certain Jesus, a Galilean deceiver, whom we crucified, but his disciples stole him by night from the tomb, where he was laid when taken down from the cross, and now deceive people by asserting that he has risen from the dead and ascended to heaven.'

This Jewish polemic against the church attested for the middle of the second century is at least just less than a century older, as Matt. 28.15 attests. For according to the information of the evangelist Matthew, down to his own day Jews are spreading the rumour that the disciples stole the body of Jesus to prove his resurrection.

(b) Celsus

Thanks to the work *Against Celsus* by the church father Origen (died c.251 CE), extracts have been preserved from an anti-Christian polemical writing composed by the educated pagan Celsus around 178 CE (Chadwick 1956 remains fundamental here). Within the framework of the passages which have been preserved, Celsus repeatedly refers to the statements of a Jewish informant. In 1.28–38 we have the assertion that the virgin birth was invented by Jesus himself. In truth he was of lowly origin and came from an adulterous relationship between his mother, who was a manual worker, and the soldier Panthera. Thereupon she had been cast out by her husband, also a manual worker, and, wandering around in disgrace, had given birth secretly to Jesus somewhere. Jesus had later gone to Egypt to work as a day labourer and there learned to use magic powers. Finally, proud of his capacities, he had returned home, where he had publicly claimed to be God.

To make things clearer, here is a translation of the key passages:

'1.28 After this Celsus represents a Jew as having a conversation with Jesus himself and refuting him on many charges, as he thinks: first, because he fabricated the story of his birth from a virgin; and he reproaches him because he came from a Jewish village and from a poor country woman who earned her living by spinning. He says that she was driven out by her husband, who was a carpenter by trade, as she was convicted of adultery. Then he says that after she had been driven out by her husband and while she was wandering about in a disgraceful way she secretly gave birth to Jesus. And he says that because he was poor he hired himself out as a workman in Egypt, and there tried his hand at certain magical powers on which the Egyptians pride themselves; he returned full of conceit because of these powers, and on account of them gave himself the title of God.'

'1.32 Let us, return, however, to the words put into the mouth of the Jew, where the mother of Jesus is described as having been turned out by the carpenter who was betrothed to her, as she had been convicted of adultery and had a child by a certain soldier named Panthera. Let us consider whether those who fabricated the myth that the virgin and Panthera committed adultery and that the carpenter turned her out, were not blind when they concocted all this to get rid of the miraculous conception by the Holy Spirit.'

'1.33. For the offspring of such impure intercourse must rather have been some stupid man who would harm men by teaching licentiousness, unrighteousness and other evils, and not a teacher of self-control, righteousness and the other virtues, 34 but, as the prophets foretold, the off-spring of a virgin who according to the promised sign should give birth to a child whose name was significant of his work, showing that at his birth God would be with men.'

Celsus' 'Jew' evidently combines the essential arguments which were presented by Jews in the second century against the supernatural birth of Jesus. Whether they go back to the first century can hardly be decided on the basis of Celsus' work alone.

In it we can generally establish a knowledge of the Gospel of Matthew (cf. 1.34/Matt. 2.2,9; 1.40/Matt. 3.16; 1.58/ Matt. 2.2, 7, 16). Moreover some elements of the section just quoted recall Matthew: cf. Joseph as a carpenter (only in Matt. 13.55); conception during the period of betrothal (only in Matt. 1.18); Jesus' stay in Egypt combined with the assertion that he is son of God (Matt. 2.15); the motif of the magicians (Matt. 2.1), though Celsus makes this negative.

However, the text deviates from the Gospel of Matthew above all on two points:

1. Joseph casts his wife out for adultery. 2. The name of the seducer is also given: he is the Roman soldier Panthera. Therefore initially the question must remain open how exten-sive and how old the tradition is on which the arguments of the Jew in Celsus are based. That it is simply a reaction to the Gospel of Matthew (thus Meier 1991: 225) is a thesis which is refuted by the evidence given.

Pornographic interpretations of the virgin birth by Jews?

Now it has been suggested from different sides that the asser-tion of the illegitimate birth of Jesus is an obvious reaction to the assertion of the virgin birth. David Friedrich Strauss sarcastically remarked: '. . . this Jewish blasphemy merely gave Christian dogma its due. Too strong a presumption must meet with an abrupt rejection; one must answer rudeness with rudeness' (Strauss 1841: 95).

This thesis is nowadays supported by two arguments: (a) similarly, the report of the theft of Jesus' body, which can be found in Matt. 28.15 and in Justin (see above, pp. 55 f.), is a reaction to the proof of the resurrection from the empty tomb; (b) the name of Jesus' father, Panthera, is simply a distortion or caricature of the term *parthenos*, the Greek word for virgin (cf. Gnilka 1986:18). Jesus the son of the *parthenos* is the son of Panthera.

On (a): This is certainly true, so that in principle a spontaneous counter-legend must always be thought possible. But since Celsus, whose work Origen for the most part reproduces, knows nothing of this legend of the theft of Jesus' corpse, caution must be exercised in any attempt to construct over-hasty analogies from this passage.

On (b): Here *first* the question who could have understood such an allusion immediately arises (cf. Maier 1978: 266), all the more so since Panthera was a well-known Greek proper name which appears on Latin inscriptions of the early Roman imperial period, particularly as the surname of Roman soldiers (cf. Schaberg 1987: 167). *Secondly*, Jesus is never called 'son of the virgin' in the Christian sources of the first two centuries. So how can it be explained plausibly that the name Panthera is a caricature of a title which was not used at all? *Thirdly*, the development would be conceivable only in Greek-speaking Judaism, since 'virgin' is a mistranslation of the Hebrew (see p. 76 below). *Fourthly*, in the early period belief in the virgin birth of Jesus was not disseminated widely, at least in Galilee. So when and where would it have arisen and immediately been caricatured? (For individual reasons see Smith 1978: 46f.). All this tells against the derivation of the name Panthera from *parthenos*.

Conclusion: In itself the Jewish charge of the illegitimate birth of Jesus cannot be dated to the first century. However, seen along with Mark 6, it might reinforce the fact that Jesus was in fact born illegitimately. In that case it possibly becomes clear *why* the Christians developed the notion of the conception of Jesus and the virgin birth at all. It was a reaction to the report, meant as a slander but historically correct, that Jesus was conceived or born outside wedlock. Of course other aspects were in play in the development of the doctrine of procreation by the Spirit and virgin birth (cf. below, pp. 72–6). But this seems to have been a plausible means of immediately relieving the illegitimate birth of Jesus of its ugliness.

The Gospel of Matthew

Matt. 1.1–17
The genealogy of Jesus

'1 *The record of the origin of Jesus Christ, the son of David, the son of Abraham.*
2   ¹Abraham was the father of Isaac,
      ² and Isaac the father of Jacob,
      ³ and Jacob the father of Judah *and his brothers*,
3   ⁴ and Judah the father of Perez and Zerah *by Tamar*,
      ⁵ and Perez the father of Hezron,
      ⁶ and Hezron the father of Ram,
      ⁷ and Ram the father of Amminadab,
      ⁸ and Amminadab the father of Nahshon,
      ⁹ and Nahshon the father of Salmon,
5   ¹⁰ and Salmon the father of Boaz *by Rahab*,
      ¹¹ and Boaz the father of Obed *by Ruth*,
      ¹² and Obed the father of Jesse,
6   ¹³ and Jesse the father of king David.
      ¹/¹⁴ And David was the father of Solomon *by the (wife) of Uriah*,
      ² and Solomon the father of Rehoboam,
      ³ and Rehoboam the father of Abijah,
      ⁴ and Abijah the father of Asa,
8   ⁵ and Asa the father of Jehoshaphat,
      ⁶ and Jehoshaphat the father of Joram,
      ⁷ and Joram the father of Uzziah,

⁸ and Uzziah the father of Jotham,
⁹ and Jotham the father of Ahaz,
¹⁰ and Ahaz the father of Hezekiah,
¹¹ and Hezekiah the father of Manasseh,
¹² and Manasseh the father of Amon,
¹³ and Amon the father of Josiah,
¹⁴ and Josiah the father of Jechoniah *and his brothers,
at the time of the deportation to Babylon.*
12 *And after the deportation to Babylon:*
¹ Jechoniah was the father of Shealtiel,
² and Shealtiel the father of Zerubbabel,
13 ³ and Zerubbabel the father of Abiud,
⁴ and Abiud the father of Eliakim,
⁵ and Eliakim the father of Azor,
14 ⁶ and Azor the father of Zadok,
⁷ and Zadok the father of Achim,
⁸ and Achim the father of Eliud,
15 ⁹ and Eliud the father of Eleazar,
¹⁰ and Eleazar the father of Matthan,
¹¹ and Matthan the father of Jacob,
16 ¹² and Jacob the father of ¹³Joseph *the husband of Mary,
of whom* Jesus was born, *who is called* ¹⁴*Christ.*
17 *All the generations from Abraham to David were
fourteen generations, and from David to the deportation to
Babylon fourteen generations, and from the deportation to
Babylon to the Christ fourteen generations.*

Redaction

[1] With 'origin', the introductory sentence anticipates 1.18.
The beginnings and endings of works by ancient authors
have great importance for them, and for us are often the key
to understanding the works. Verse 1 refers to the genealogy
in 1.2–16 or to the introductory chapter of the Gospel. In
shaping the beginning of his Gospel Matthew is influenced by
Mark 1.1 and develops Jesus' descent and at the same time
his future.

[2–16a] The genealogy consists of a series of monotonous, brief, main clauses. Additional redactional comments have been inserted into them: wives (vv.3, 5ab, 6b, cf. v.16), brothers (vv.2c, 11), David as king (v.6a), and twice the exile. [16b] Jesus Christ is the goal of this genealogy. The expression 'Jesus who is called Christ' appears in the passion narrative word for word on the lips of Pilate (Matt. 27.17), who wants to release Jesus despite bitter Jewish opposition because he is convinced of his innocence. In breaking up the scheme of the genealogy, which laconically cites one father after another, and speaking of Mary 'of whom Jesus was born', using the same verb in the passive, he excludes Joseph as Jesus' father. By so doing he prepares readers for the following narrative of the procreation of Jesus from the spirit of God and his birth from the virgin Mary. At the same time the text shows that the evangelist is aware of the suspicion of illegitimacy which lies over Jesus (cf. Schaberg 1987: 35f.). Some textual witnesses have nevertheless introduced Joseph directly as father in v.16b. But the translation above is certainly based on the original text of Matthew.

[17] This verse deciphers the redactional division. The genealogy consists of three times fourteen generations. If the genealogy extends only to Joseph, for this scheme to work David and the Babylonian exile have to be counted twice. But since Christ is explicitly mentioned in v.17, *he* is probably the fourteenth member of the series; in that case the Babylonian exile counts only once.

The division into three times fourteen might be Matthew's work. Seven ($14 = 2 \times 7$) is a symbolic number which often appears in the Gospel:

7 demons Matt. 12.45
7 loaves Matt. 15.34
7 baskets Matt. 15.37
7 x forgiveness Matt. 18.21f.
7 brothers Matt. 22.25
7 woes Matt. 23

Of the passages mentioned here, Matt. 12.45 and Matt. 23 appear only in the first Gospel. Matthew 15.34, 37 and 22.25 have been taken over from Mark, whereas Matt. 18.21f. derives from the Sayings Source Q.

Jesus as son of David and son of Abraham

The evangelist gives the traditional genealogy different goals. Two of them are found in the heading in v.1 alone. This names Jesus both son of David and son of Abraham.

As *son of David,* Jesus is king of Israel. So in v.6 the author might have emphasized David as king. In the very next chapter (2.1–12), Jesus is the counterpart of king Herod, and in 21.11 he then enters Jerusalem as the other, gentle, king (cf. 21.5).

As *son of Abraham,* Jesus is part of the secret theme of the Matthaean infancy narrative, the inclusion of the Gentiles in an expanded, new Israel. (In Judaism, Abraham is the symbol of the proselyte, since in him all the generations of the earth are to be blessed; cf. Gen.12.3.) This aspect is also expressed in the women of the genealogy, who are all of Gentile origin. This and their relationship to the fifth woman, Mary, needs to be explained.

The four women in the genealogy

(a) None of the women is Jewish (cf. the basic comments in Stegemann 1971 and Nolland 1997 for a survey of research). Granted, *Tamar's* origin is not mentioned explicitly anywhere in the Old Testament. But Jewish tradition generally mentions her as a daughter of Aram (cf. Jub.41.4), i.e. she is regarded as an Aramaean (cf. Johnson 1988: 154). In 4.12 the book of Ruth makes her parallel with Ruth (whose house is to become 'like the house of Perez, whom Tamar bore to Judah') and thus suggests that she is not of Israelite origin. *Ruth* is a Moabite woman. *Rahab* lived in the Canaanite city of Jericho (Josh.2.1). *Bathsheba* is not mentioned by name but is merely introduced as the wife of Uriah. Now he was a Hittite (cf. II Sam. 11.3). As the daughter of Eliam (ibid.), whose name is attested only as Israelite, she herself was certainly of Jewish origin; but by her marriage to Uriah the Hittite, for Matthew at least she became a 'Gentile'. For in ancient Judaism, if a woman married a man of another origin she adopted his religion (cf. Stegemann 1971: 261). This practice is still current in the Orient.

We can hardly interpret this evidence to mean that in Matthew's view the fifth woman in the genealogy, Mary, was also not Jewish. That already comes to grief on her purely Jewish name Mary (= Hebrew Miriam). Rather, the four non-Jewish women in the genealogy seem to be a concealed indication that the Messiah of Israel is at the same time the one who also brings salvation to the Gentiles. This is then explicitly emphasized at the end of the Gospel, where the disciples are given the task of making disciples of all nations (Matt. 28.19f.). Through Christ, the son of Abraham, in the new covenant they too come to share in being true children of Abraham. The story of the adoration of the magicians which immediately follows (Matt. 2) similarly emphasizes the notion of Jesus' concern for the Gentiles (see p. 82 below).

(b) But what is the relationship between the four women of the genealogy and the fifth woman, if they do not all have in common the fact that they are not Jewish? This question is all the more urgent, since Mary must be in some relationship to the four other women in the genealogy. (This is where the favourite view of the four female ancestors of the Messiah Jesus as types of Mary is right.) Otherwise it would be too great a coincidence that, contrary to practice, women were inserted into a genealogy *and* that at the end of the genealogy again there was a woman in place of a man.

The four women in the genealogy have two things in common.

First, their action could have been offensive to Jewish sensibilities: *Tamar*'s children were born in blood guilt (Gen. 38); *Rahab* was a harlot (Josh. 2.1); *Ruth* got her second husband only through sexual provocation (Ruth 3.4, 7–9, 12–13); and *Bathsheba*'s relationship with David began with adultery (II Sam. 11.4). The fact that Matthew does not speak of Bathsheba but of 'the (wife) of Uriah' probably indicates that he is not thinking of David's later wife but of the act of adultery (cf. Schaberg 1987: 22).

Secondly, the text sees all four as heroines who through their male partners Judah, Salmon, Boaz and David became ancestors of the Messiah.

Initially Joseph, the husband of the fifth woman, Mary, is open to the same misunderstanding as could have arisen among the innocent readers of the narratives about the four other women. However, through the revelation of an angel he is led to a correct understanding.

This interpretation of the texts fits well with the evidence that Jews spoke of the illegitimate birth of Jesus from Mary. Matthew explains this blemish in Mary by referring to the above-mentioned four women in the genealogy, who only *seemed* to have a blemish.

Tradition

The genealogy, which probably derives from tradition – otherwise Matthew would have compiled it himself – belongs to the type of 'unilinear' genealogies (without branches) which in antiquity often served to provide legitimation (there are examples of genealogies with branches, for example in I Chron. 1.1–5.17; 7; 8). It focusses on Joseph as Jesus' father and is meant to indicate that Jesus is descended from the patriarch Abraham through the royal dynasty of Israel. He is not only a true Jew but a son of David.

For an example of another genealogy of Jesus see Luke 3.23–38 (see below, pp. 119–22).

History

For a clarification of the historicity of the genealogy cf. the remarks on Luke 3.23–38 (see below, pp. 121 f.).

The announcement of the birth of Jesus

'18 *Now the origin of Jesus Christ took place in this way* [and not otherwise]:

When his mother Mary had been betrothed to Joseph, before they came together she was found to be pregnant of holy spirit [and not by another man]. 19 Joseph, her husband, who was a just man and did not want to put her to shame, resolved to divorce her quietly.

20 But after he had considered this, behold, an angel of the Lord appeared to him in a dream, saying, "Joseph, son of David, do not fear to take Miriam your wife, for that which is conceived in her is of holy spirit; 21 she will bear a son, and you shall call his name Jesus, for he will save his people from their sins."

22 *Now all this took place to fulfil what the Lord had spoken by the prophet:* 23 "Behold, the virgin shall become pregnant and bear a son, and his name shall be called Immanuel", *which being translated means, God is with us.*

24 When Joseph woke from sleep, he did as the angel of the Lord commanded him; he took his wife. 25 *And he did not know her until she had borne a son; and he called his name Jesus.*'

Redaction

[18] The title sentence ('origin') refers back to vv. 1 and 16 and comes from the final redactor. He began his work with v.1: 'The record of the *origin* of Jesus Christ, the son of David, the son of Abraham.' After listing the genealogy from Abraham to Joseph (vv.2–16a), in v.16b he goes over to the story of the birth which now follows. The transition is clumsy, because the story in Matt. 1.18–25 will show the Holy Spirit as the father of Jesus, whereas the genealogy leads us to expect Joseph as father. Matthew resolves this difficulty

66

by stating that the procreation of Jesus was from Mary (and not through Joseph, see above, pp. 61 f.). Nevertheless Joseph takes his pregnant fiancée into his house and legitimates her son by naming him himself (Matt. 1.20f.,24f.). Thus Jesus has been adopted into the wider family of the house of David (just as, for example, his Roman contemporary Octavian, the later emperor Augustus, was accepted into the *gens Julia* by Caesar through adoption). So there is no longer a contradiction between genealogy and birth narrative.

[18b] The observation that Mary is pregnant 'of holy spirit' anticipates the instruction that Joseph will first be given by the angel (20) and really breaks the narrative tension too early. The anticipatory reference to the procreation by the Holy Spirit presupposes that the readers have information. In anticipation, by reinforcing v.18a, it is meant *once again* to repudiate the Jewish accusation that Jesus was conceived out of wedlock. Thus the reader already knows what Joseph learns only in v.20: the procreation of Jesus is through the Holy Spirit.

It is striking that the conception of Jesus is not related directly, but only its consequences. This too is a further point of contact for the suspicion that Matthew is responding to attacks which allude to the questionable origin of Jesus as a child conceived pre-maritally (and/or in fornication).

[19] Here Joseph, who is betrothed to Mary and thus legally married, moves into the centre of the event. At that time the period between betrothal and wedding, during which the couple should not yet have had sexual intercourse, usually lasted from six to twelve months. For this period the young bride-to-be, who was between twelve and fourteen years old, still lived in her parents' house (for this and other technicalities of marriage at that time see Archer 1990: 123–206). However, she was already regarded as the man's wife and therefore could theoretically also become a widow (cf. Billerbeck II, 393f.). Joseph has to suspect Mary of adultery because of her pregnancy and therefore wants to let her go, i.e. divorce her.

In cases of adultery, in addition – at least theoretically – there were two further possible ways to proceed:

- A 'water of cursing ritual' as a divine verdict when there is *suspicion of adultery* (Num. 5.11–31): the priest offers the woman suspected of adultery 'holy water', which is mixed with some earth from the floor of the sanctuary. In addition the woman pronounces a curse on herself. If the suspicion is correct, this self-inflicted curse will work and the water will produce deformities of the lower part of the body which prove her guilt. These archaic-sounding regulations, in which probably a number of procedures, each originally thought of as automatic, have been amalgamated (cf. Noth 1968: 49), may stem from ancient practice. However, it is very questionable whether they were used in the first century,
- The stoning of those involved in a case of *proven adultery* (Deut. 22.23f.): '23 If there is a betrothed virgin, and a man meets her in the city and lies with her, 24 then you shall bring them both out to the gate of that city, and you shall stone them to death with stones, the young woman because she did not cry for help though she was in the city, and the man because he violated his neighbour's wife; so you shall purge the evil from the midst of you.' Here it is presupposed that the girl is also guilty because she has not appealed to the legal protection of the community.

An actual rape is therefore possible only outside the city (Deut. 22.25–27):

'25 But if in the open country a man meets a young woman who is betrothed, and the man seizes her and lies with her, then only the man who lay with her shall die. 26 But to the young woman you shall do nothing; in the young woman there is no offence punishable by death, for this case is like that of a man attacking and murdering his neighbour; 27 because he came upon her in the open country, and though the betrothed young woman cried for help there was no one to rescue her.'

How the partner of the raped fiancée or wife is to behave towards her is not explicitly said.

In the case of the rape of a woman who is not betrothed, the man is merely compelled to take the young woman after paying the usual bride price for his wife (Deut. 22.28f.).

The three following texts illustrate the scorn to which women who had a pre-marital or extra-marital relationship were exposed at that time, and the shame which fell on any child who happened to be born to them:

Sir.23.23–26: '23 For first of all, she (viz., a wife who has deceived her husband) has disobeyed the law of the Most High; second, she has committed an offence against her husband; and thirdly, she has committed adultery through harlotry and brought forth children by another man. 24 Such a woman will be brought before the assembly, and punishment will fall upon her children. 25 Her children will not take root, and her branches will not bear fruit. 26. When people remember her they will curse her, and her disgrace will never be blotted out.'

Wisdom 3.16–19: '16 But children of adulterers will not come to maturity, and the offspring of an unlawful union will perish. 17 For even if they live long they will be held of no account, and finally their old age will be without honour. 18 If they die young, they will have no hope and no consolation in the day of decision. 19 For the end of an unrighteous generation is grievous.'

Wisdom 4.3–6: '3 But the prolific brood of the ungodly will be of no use, and none of their illegitimate seedlings will strike a deep root or take a firm hold. 4. For even if they put forth boughs for a while, standing insecurely they will be shaken by the wind, and by the violence of the winds they will be uprooted. 5 The branches will be broken off before they come to maturity, and their fruit will be useless, not ripe enough to eat, and good for nothing. 6 For children born of unlawful unions are witnesses of evil against their parents when God examines them.'

Back to the text of Matthew: Joseph chose a mild form of separation. Matthew describes him as 'just'. This indicates his friendly disposition (cf. Matt. 25.37; 10.41; 13.41) and explains his intention not to put his wife to shame. At the same time, doing God's will plays a part in being just; for example, it did not in any way allow the acceptance of illegitimate children into the family.

[20] As v.18a already indicated, Matthew is concerned to explain the implantation of the virgin's son in the family of David. The way in which Joseph is addressed as 'son of David' takes up the superscription in 1.1, where Jesus is called son of David. Only at this point in the New Testament is someone other than Jesus called son of David – an indication of how important the figure of Joseph is for Matthew.

[21] The explanation of the name Jesus indicates the future task of the Messiah: 'He will save his people from their sins.' The forgiveness of sins takes place in Matthew's community (cf. 26.28). Matthew 2.6 makes the term 'people' more specific: it is 'my people Israel'. However, in the Gospel 'people' has predominantly negative connotations (cf. 13.15; 15.8; 27.25) or denotes a distant relationship to Jesus, e.g. in the formula 'the high priests and elders of the people' (26.47; 27.1; cf. 21.23; 2.4). Thus in Matt. 1.21 Matthew is thinking of the new people of God.

[22f.] The fulfilment quotation, according to which the newborn child is to be called 'Immanuel', interprets 'all this' as the fulfilment of a prophetic prediction, indeed as a saying which the Lord himself has spoken through the prophet (Isa. 7.14). (The LXX version which underlies the quotation mistranslates *almah* [= young woman] by *parthenos* [= virgin].) The translation of Immanuel as 'God with us' points to the promise of the risen Christ that he will be with the community (28.20). 'The presence of the exalted Lord in his community proves that he is Immanuel, God with us' (Luz 1992: 105).

[24f.] These verses narrate the execution of what is commanded in v.20: Joseph takes his wife and therefore does not dismiss her, as according to v.19 he had initially planned.

[25] The fact that Joseph has no sexual intercourse with Mary before the birth of the child makes it clear that here no man was indeed involved. This verse does not yet envisage the later church view that Joseph did not sleep with Mary even after the birth of Jesus (the perpetual virginity of Mary).

Conclusion: one important aim of the story is *theological*. Jesus is the Immanuel. Thus right from the beginning Matthew points to the living reality of the community with which Jesus is always, to the end of the world (28.16–20). If 28.16–20 tell us that the risen Christ is none other than the earthly Jesus and that being a Christian means keeping his commandments, 1.18–15 make it clear that the earthly Jesus is none other than the exalted Christ who is with his community. At the same time, right at the beginning the Gospel of Matthew – and that is relevant in this Gospel of the law and the commandments – contains a clear reference to the grace which has taken place through Jesus Christ.

Furthermore, the narrative has an *ethical* aspect, which relates to the figure of the just Joseph and his obedience.

It is also important as a story, because in it an Old Testament prophecy is fulfilled. To this degree, and only to this degree, the virgin birth is also significant. Here it is not regarded as purification from unclean sexuality. It is a further explanation of the implantation of Jesus in the family of David which was left open in 1.16. To exaggerate, one could say that Jesus is a member of the house of David *despite* the virgin birth, which is known to the community.

This episode too, however, is also rooted in controversy and was narrated by Matthew in order to repudiate hostile Jewish rumours about the shady circumstances of Jesus' birth, i.e. to explain the true state of affairs:

71

'Anyone will think that the virgin birth is reported in 1.18–25 in the most remarkable way conceivable. All we are told is that Joseph found Mary pregnant before the beginning of their life together and was required by an angel nevertheless to accept as his wife a Mary who was pregnant by the Holy Spirit. Does one report such a great divine wonder like that?' (Hirsch 1941: 325).

Tradition

A precise outline or even a form of the tradition can hardly be reconstructed, since Matthew has worked over the story comprehensively. However, the following elements of tradition can be identified:

(a) The pregnancy of Mary without the involvement of Joseph;

(b) The procreation of Jesus by the Holy Spirit and – connected with this –

(c) The birth of Jesus from the virgin Mary (also based on the LXX translation of *almah* [Isa.7.14] in the sense of *bethulah* [= virgin])

Divine sonship – procreation by the Spirit – virgin birth

How did it come about that Christians imagined the origin of Jesus in this way? On pp. 59 f. it became clear that the statement that the procreation of Jesus was by the Holy Spirit and that he was born of a virgin virtually offered itself to them as a reaction to Jewish criticism about Jesus' illegitimate birth. After all, here they could refer back to notions which had already been developed long beforehand in their religious environment.

The transfer of these notions to Jesus was particularly favoured by the confession that Jesus was the *Son of God*. Jesus was already given this title in the primitive community: according to the Jewish Christian traditions underlying Rom.1.3f. his institution as son of God took place through

72

the resurrection (see above, p. 45). The divine sonship of Jesus is also understood in this sense in an old formula which Luke reproduces in Acts 13.32f.: 'And we bring you the good news that what God promised to the fathers, this he has fulfilled to us their children by raising Jesus; as also it is written in the second psalm, "Your are my son, today I have begotten you" (Ps.2.7).' By contrast, the Gospel of Mark contains a tradition which to some degree brings the divine sonship forward: here Jesus already becomes Son of God in connection with the baptism (Mark 1.11).

Now this very designation 'Son of God' was also current in the Hellenistic world – but with quite a different significance. What was understood by it when e.g. Heracles, Pythagoras, Plato, Pharaohs, Alexander the Great, Scipio Africanus maior and the emperor Augustus were designated sons of God (cf. the examples in Braun 1971: 256) is already evident from the notion that is mainly associated with it: the Son of God is *fathered* by a God.

True, the fathering is usually understood in a crudely objective sense; but there are also instances of an interpretation of the procreation in a more sublime, spiritualized sense. Thus Plutarch (c. 50–120 CE) writes:

'And there is some reason for supposing that Deity, who is not a lover of horses or birds, but a lover of men, should be willing to consort with men of superlative goodness, and should not dislike or disdain the company of a wise and holy man. But that an immortal god should take carnal pleasure in a mortal and mortal beauty, this, surely, is hard to believe. 4 And yet the Egyptians make a distinction here which is thought plausible, namely that while a woman can be approached by a divine spirit, there is no such thing as carnal intercourse or communion between a man and a divinity' (*Numa* 4,3f.).

Birth from a virgin is no more a genuinely Christian notion than procreation by the spirit. Two feasts are attested in

Egypt in Christian times which glorify the birth of a child of God from a virgin. (a) A festival of Aion which was celebrated in Alexandria on the night of 5/6 January had its climax in a procession involving an image of the God. When asked about the meaning of the celebration, those who knew replied: 'At this hour, today, the Kore, that is the virgin, gave birth to the Aion' (Epiphanius, *Haer.* 51, 22, 10). (b) On 25 December, at a celebration of the festival of the winter solstice, the celebrants cried out, 'The virgin has given birth, the light is increasing' (cf. Norden 1969: 24–33).

Philo of Alexandria (c.15 BCE–45 CE) attests that such notions were not alien to Hellenistic Judaism either when in his allegorical exposition of the marriages of Abraham, Jacob, Isaac and Moses he interprets their wives Sarah, Leah, Rebecca and Zipporah as virtues:

> '43 Thus then must the sacred instruction begin. Man and woman, male and female of the human race, in the course of nature come together to hold intercourse for the procreation of children. But virtues whose offspring are so many and so perfect may not have to do with mortal man, yet if they receive no seed of generation from another they will never of themselves conceive. 44 Who then is he that sows in them the good seed save the Father of all, that is God unbegotten and begetter of all things? He then sows, but the fruit of his sowing, the fruit which is his own, he bestows as a gift. For God begets nothing for himself, for he is in want of nothing, but all for him who needs to receive.
>
> 45 I will give as a warrant for my words one that none can dispute, Moses the holiest of men. For he shows us Sarah conceiving at the time when God visited her in her solitude, but when she brings forth it is not to the author of her visitation, but to him who seeks to win wisdom, whose name is Abraham.
>
> 46 And even clearer is Moses' teaching of Leah, that God opened her womb (Gen. 29. 31). Now to open the womb

belongs to the husband. Yet when she conceived she brought forth not to God (for he is in himself all-sufficing for himself), but to him who endures toil to gain the good, even Jacob. Thus virtue receives the divine seed from the (divine) author, but brings forth to one of her own lovers, who is preferred above all others who seek her favour.

47 Again Isaac the all-wise besought God, and through the power of him who was thus besought Steadfastness or Rebecca became pregnant (Gen. 25.21). And without supplication or entreaty did Moses, when he took Zipporah the winged and soaring virtue, find her pregnant through no mortal agency (Ex. 2.22) . . .

49 . . . Thus he (viz. the prophet Jeremiah) . . . proclaimed an oracle in the name of God to Virtue the all-peaceful. 'Did you not call me your house, the father and the husband of your virginity?' (Jer. 3.4). Thus he teaches us quite clearly that God is a house, the incorporeal dwelling-place of incorporeal ideas, that God is the father of all things, for he begat them, and the husband of Wisdom, dropping the seed of happiness for the race of mortals into good and virgin soil. 50 For it is fitting that God should hold converse with the truly virgin nature, that which is undefiled and free from impure touch; but it is the opposite with us. For the union of human beings that is made for the procreation of children, turns virgins into women. But when God begins to consort with the soul, he makes what before was a woman into a virgin again, for he takes away the degenerate and emasculated passions which unmanned it and plants instead the native growth of unpolluted virtues. Thus he will not talk with Sarah till she has ceased from all that is after the manner of women (Gen. 18. 11), and is ranked once more as a pure virgin (*On the Cherubim* 43–50; Loeb Classical Library translation, Vol. 2, pp.35–39).

Conclusion: The notion that Jesus was fathered by the Holy Spirit and born of a virgin derives from the reinterpretation which was being given, indeed which had to be given, to the title 'son of God' at the moment when Hellenistic Jewish Christianity was making Jesus as Son of God at home in a Hellenistic environment. On the basis of this terminology, divine sonship was an ideal help towards understanding between Jewish Christians and Hellenists, though probably each party meant something quite different by it. Whereas other titles which expressed the significance of Jesus were no longer understood and either dropped ('Son of Man' no longer appears in the Pauline communities) or transformed (the title 'Messiah' becomes a proper name in the Greek form 'Christ'), the designation 'son of God' took on a completely new content: now 'son of God ' is no longer understood as a title of Jesus but as a statement about his natural quality, i.e. is interpreted in a physical sense. By legend he was then associated with a virgin who alone was regarded worthy of God.

In the process of the reinterpretation of divine sons the fact that already in Hellenism the milder assumption of a fathering by the Spirit had been developed in place of a crudely objective notion of divine fathering may have played a major role. This middle way must have been particularly attractive for Hellenistic Jewish Christians. For them it was inconceivable that God should have physical dealings with a human woman. By contrast, the assumption that it was God's 'Spirit' which had fathered Jesus formed an appropriate point of contact for putting Jesus on a level with other great men whose fathering was similarly attributed to God. However, that was possible only because people no longer had a command of Hebrew, in which spirit (= *ruach*) is feminine. Cf. already the protest, impotent though it is, of the heretical Gospel of Philip against the church's exposition: 'Some say: "Mary conceived by the Holy Spirit." . . . They do not know what they are saying! When did a woman ever conceive by a woman?' (17a). A defective command of Hebrew also accounts for the quotation of Isa.7.14 as a proof text for Jesus' birth from a virgin (see p. 59 above).

The fathering of Jesus by the Holy Spirit and his birth from the Virgin Mary are unhistorical:

(a) There are numerous parallels in the history of religion which similarly deal with sons of God who are miraculously fathered and born (cf. Petersen 1909; Norden 1969).

(b) The fathering of Jesus by the Spirit and his virgin birth are only rarely attested in the New Testament and moreover in late strata of the tradition.

(c) If there was a wish to regard the virgin birth as historical, it had to be assumed that Mary only reported her intimate experiences after a long silence. However, what the earliest Synoptic tradition reports about the family of Jesus tells against this (cf. above, pp. 46–8, on Mark 3.21).

(d) But the historicity of the birth of Jesus from a virgin is also ruled out for scientific reasons. The objections made to this from the feminist side (cf. Wex 1992) tend rather to raise a smile, and are only a peripheral phenomenon within feminism.

By contrast, what emerges as a historical fact behind Matt. 1.18–25 is a hostile report which was being spread by non-Christian Jews about the illegitimate birth of Jesus. That is the real nucleus of Matthew's story. In that case it is also clear that the fathering of Jesus by an unknown man must be considered a further historical element (cf. Schaberg 1987: 41).

Rape or misdemeanour on the part of Mary?

How did the 'virgin' get the child Jesus if Joseph was not the father? Here Jewish polemic speaks a clear language, and if we make some deletions, here too it seems to be on the right track. However, a sexual misdemeanour on the part of Mary, which it presupposes, may be ruled out, since in that case Joseph would hardly have taken his fiancée Mary into his house. Moreover it should be noted that the Jewish patriarchal structure of Mary's family and her presumed age at the time of marriage (between twelve and fourteen) hardly make a sexual adventure probable. Therefore, shocking though this may seem at first glance, the assumption that Mary was raped almost forces itself upon us as an explanation of this dark streak in her history and in the history of her son Jesus. (This thesis was first developed by Schaberg in 1987 – in part using other arguments.)

The general objection may be made that in that case Mary would no longer have been acceptable as the Jewish mother of a large family. Mark 6.3 and I Cor.9.5 indeed presuppose the existence of brothers and sisters of Jesus. But sexual blemishes on women, which included rape, were important in the Judaism of that time only in the case of marriage with a priest (and Joseph was not a priest). For example, a former prisoner of war could not become the wife of a priest, because here the possibility of rape could not be ruled out. Josephus writes this about it in his *Antiquities*:

'From the priests Moses exacted a double degree of purity. He forbade them to wed a harlot, he forbids them to wed a slave or a prisoner of war or such women as earn their living by hawking or innkeeping or who have for whatsoever reason been cast off by their former husbands' (III, 276)

These regulations are connected with the exegesis of Lev. 21.13f.: 'And he (viz. the high priest) shall take a wife in her virginity. A widow, or one divorced, or a woman who has been defiled, or a harlot, these he shall not marry; but he shall take to wife a virgin of his own people.' Cf. also the fact narrated by Josephus, *Antt.* XIII, 291f., that John Hyrcanus (died 104 BCE) was told by the Pharisee Eleazar that he had to resign from the high priesthood because his mother had been a prisoner of war in the reign of Antiochus Epiphanes (175–164 BCE) (and therefore possibly had been raped: see Archer 1990: 138f.).

Now against the reconstruction proposed here it could be pointed out that had Mary been raped, according to Jewish law she remained innocent and therefore the expression 'son of Mary' was unjustified. For if a rape is not a blemish, Jesus could not have been denigrated by the designation 'son of Mary'. Theoretically that is correct. But the modern distinction between law and morality in fact already existed at that time. Arguments were resorted to in the controversy which may not have been legitimate but which were all the more effective – and these always have to do with sexuality (cf. the examples in Lüdemann 1996: 86 [Paul], 159 [Marcion]).

Matt. 2.1–23
The magicians from the East and Herod's infanticide

'1 Now when Jesus was born in Bethlehem in Judaea in the days of Herod the king, behold, magicians from the East came to Jerusalem, saying, 2 "Where is the newborn king of the Jews? For we have seen his star in the East, and have come to worship him."
3 When Herod the king heard this, he was troubled, and all Jerusalem with him; 4 and assembling all the chief priests and scribes of the people, he enquired of them where the Christ was to be born. 5 They told him, "In Bethlehem of Judaea; for so it is written by the prophet: 6 And you, O Bethlehem, in the land of Judah, are by no means least among the rulers of Judah; for from you shall come a ruler who will govern my people Israel."
7 Then Herod summoned the magicians secretly and ascertained from them precisely when the star appeared; 8 and he sent them to Bethlehem, saying, "Go and search diligently for the child, and when you have found him bring me word, that I too may come and worship him."
9 When they had heard the king they went their way. And behold, the star which they had seen in the East went before them, till it came to rest over the place where the

child was. 10 When they saw the star, they rejoiced exceedingly.

11 And they went into the house and saw the child with Mary his mother, and they fell down and worshiped him and opened their treasures and offered him their gifts, gold and frankincense and myrrh.

12 And they received a prophecy in a dream not to return to Herod, and departed to their own country by another way.

13 Now when they had departed, behold, an angel of the Lord appeared to Joseph in a dream and said, "Rise, take the child and his mother, and flee to Egypt, and remain there till I tell you; for Herod is about to search for the child, to destroy him." 14 And he rose and took the child and his mother by night, and departed to Egypt, 15 and remained there until the death of Herod. *This was to fulfil what the Lord had spoken by the prophet,* "Out of Egypt have I called my son."

16 When Herod saw that he had been tricked by the magicians, he became very angry, and he sent and had all the male children in Bethlehem and in all that region who were two years old or under killed, according to the time which he had ascertained from the magicians. 17 *Then was fulfilled what was spoken by the prophet Jeremiah*: 18 "A voice was heard in Ramah, wailing and loud lamentation, Rachel weeping for her children; she refused to be consoled, because they were no more."

19 But when Herod had died, behold, an angel of the Lord appeared in a dream to Joseph in Egypt, and said, 20 "Arise, take the child and his mother, and go to the land of Israel, for those who sought the child's life are dead."

21 And he rose and took the child and his mother, and went to the land of Israel. 22 But when he heard that Archelaus reigned over Judaea in place of his father Herod, he was afraid to go there, and being warned in a dream he withdrew to the district of Galilee. 23 And he went and dwelt in a city called Nazareth, *that what was*

spoken by the prophets might be fulfilled, "He shall be called a Nazorene."'

General

This text is independent of the section 1.18–25 and does not presuppose it. Moreover it is not itself a unity, since the combination of the story of the magicians and that of the infanticide is certainly secondary and derives from an unhistorical link which is rooted in dogmatics. The author depicts a sacred past which is governed by the notion of the fulfilment of Old Testament prophecies. The birth in Egypt, the stay in Egypt, the journey to Nazareth – all this is backed up with quotations from the Old Testament (vv.6, 15, 18, 23) which are now generally abandoned as real prophecies (cf. the remarks about this in the next section).

Moreover, even where the author needs the vengeance of Herod to emphasize the deliverance of the Christ child, he does not hesitate to look in the Old Testament for a basis for this treacherous action. It should be emphasized in advance that all this is sheer invention, which is made even worse by the elaboration of a horrific infanticide. David Friedrich Strauss rightly asked more than 150 years ago: 'But if it be once admitted that God interposed supernaturally to blind the mind of Herod and to suggest to the magicians that they should not return to Jerusalem, we are constrained to ask, why did not God in the first instance inspire the magicians to shun Jerusalem and proceed to Bethlehem, whither Herod's attention would not then have been so immediately attracted, and thus the disastrous sequel perhaps have been altogether avoided?' (1972: 165).

Division

A. The magicians (vv.1–12)
   a. Arrival of the magicians in Jerusalem (vv.1f.)
   b. Privy council in Jerusalem (vv.3–6)
   c. Interrogation of the magicians (vv.7f.)

    d. The magicians travel to Bethlehem (vv.9f.)
    e. Adoration by the magicians (v.11)
    f. Return of the magicians (v.12)
B. Flight of Joseph's family to Egypt (vv.13–15)
C. Herod's infanticide (vv.16–18)
D. Return of the family from Egypt (vv.19–23)

The scene of the first three subdivisions of the story of the magicians is Jerusalem; the last two take place in Jerusalem. The individual parts are held together *first* by the twofold journey and arrival of the magicians (vv.1,9), *secondly* by the motif of the star (vv.2,9f), *thirdly* by the contrast between King Herod and the King of the Jews (vv.1f.), and *fourthly* by the contrast between Herod and the magicians, whose intention to worship the new king (v.2, carried out in v.11), Herod hypocritically takes up (v.8).

Redaction

[1] This indicates the situation and links the present narrative with 1.18–25. The birth of Jesus in Bethlehem to which 1.25 looks forward and on which 2.1 looks back is not really narrated. The readers know that the magicians (this term is used in a positive sense here, in contrast to the negative usage otherwise customary in early Christianity, as for example in Acts 13.6–8) are Gentiles. That emerges from the fact that :
[2] They paraphrase the messianic expectation known to them and enquire about the birthplace, not of the king of Israel, but of the king of the Jews.
[3] The magicians are met by Herod the Great (37–4 BCE) and 'all Jerusalem with him', who react in shock, since they have understood the message. From now on – contrary to the historical facts (Herod the Great was unpopular with the people) – Herod and all the people of Jerusalem form the Jewish front which rejects the new royal child. Their behaviour seems all the more abhorrent since they themselves know the real significance of the star. In this way Matthew

gives a foretaste of what will take place in the passion narrative and after the 'resurrection'. There at the end of the Gospel the Jewish people will say, 'His blood be upon us and upon our children' (27.25), and the Jewish leaders, though they know better, will suppress the news of the 'resurrection' by bribing the Roman soldiers (cf. 28.11–15).

[4] This verse endorses what has been said: Herod gathers all the high priests and scribes, who are pointedly termed scribes of the people (in Matthew, *laos* always denotes the Jewish people). The combination of Jesus' opponents into groups of two is typical of Matthew. The high priests, who later appear as the key initiators of the execution of Jesus, and the scribes as stubborn opponents of Jesus in his activity, also appear together in 20.18 and 21.15.

[5f.] Herod asks them about the birthplace of the Messiah. The scribes answer the king's question with the prophet Micah, 5.1: Bethlehem in Judaea is the birthplace. Matthew agrees with that, but here avoids using his fulfilment formula (cf. vv.15, 17, 23) since the hostile scribes are speaking. Although the Jewish scribes recognize that this is the expected messianic shepherd of the people of God, they go off to Herod. Here we have an anti-Jewish point made by Matthew, the final redactor.

[7] The secret interrogation of the magicians by the king points forward to v.16, which is couched in similar terms.

[8] This verse serves to show Herod up as a hypocrite. He does not at all want to worship the child, but to murder it.

[9f.] As in related accounts, here too the readers are to detect God's guidance, which is at work in the whole event.

[11] This forms the climax of the story: the magicians find the child and its mother in the house, worship it and bring it precious gifts.

[12] This rounds off the story. The child Jesus remains safe. In a dream the magicians are instructed not to return to Jerusalem. One could only have wished that this instruction had been 'vouchsafed earlier, so as to avert the steps of the

magicians from Jerusalem, and thus perchance prevent the whole subsequent massacre' (Strauss 1972: 167).

[13–15] These verses report the flight into Egypt. The narrative is very terse and inculcates two notions: God's guidance alone, God's plan which is expressed in the fulfilment quotation (cf. Hos.11.1), rescues the small child.

[16f.] The description of the cruel infanticide in Bethlehem forms a dark foil to this and emphatically expresses the actual threat to Jesus.

[17f.] Through a fulfilment quotation from Jer.31.15 these verses indicate that the cruel event, too, corresponds with the divine plan. Originally the 'prophecy' supposed to have been fulfilled by this infanticide referred to the deportation of the people of Judah to Babylon: there was no thought in it of an event lying in a distant future (Strauss 1972: 168).

[19–21] These verses, which are very similar in language to v.13f. and thus show themselves to be a redactional link, narrate the rounding off of the divine plan and bring Jesus, the son of David and Abraham, back into the land of the people to whom he is sent.

[22f.] These verses have been entirely composed by Matthew, as is shown by the parallel to them in Matt. 4.12–13. As Matthew needed an Old Testament quotation for Jesus' home town, he filled this gap himself forcibly and understood Nazorene, contrary to its meaning, as an inhabitant of Nazareth.

Tradition

Preliminary comment: since the exegesis has shown that the text has been shaped throughout by Matthew, it is difficult to extract a clearly defined text on which this was based. Therefore the task of an analysis of the tradition is to work out motifs and models on the basis of which Matthew may have composed the story.

A Roman historian of the time of Augustus reports a miraculous star at the birth and accession of Mithridates VI the Great (c.132–63 BCE):

'His future greatness was even proclaimed in advance by miraculous heavenly signs. In the year in which he was born and also in the year in which he first began to reign, during the twofold period a comet shone for seventy days, so brightly that it seemed to make the whole heaven glow. For not only did it occupy the fourth part of the heavens with its magnitude, but the gleam which flashed forth from it even surpassed the splendour of the sun; and it occupied the period of four hours each time it rose and set' (Justinus, *Epitome from Pompeius Trogus* 37,2).

Cf. also the two following reports by the imperial biographer Suetonius (born c. 70 CE):

'Caesar died in the fifty-sixth year of his age and was numbered among the gods, not only by a formal decree but also in the conviction of the common people. For at the first of the games which his heir Augustus gave in honour of his apotheosis, a comet shone for seven successive days, rising about the eleventh hour, and was believed to be the soul of Caesar, who had been taken up into heaven' (Suetonius, *Caesar*, 88).

'It chanced that a comet had begun to appear on successive nights, a thing which is commonly believed to portend the death of great rulers. Warned by this and learning from the astrologer Balbillus that kings usually averted such omens by the death of some distinguished man, thus turning from themselves upon the heads of the nobles, he resolved on the death of all the eminent men of the state' (Suetonius, *Nero* 36).

There are similarly a large number of parallels to the story of Herod wanting to kill the new-born king. The motif appears both in the Old Testament saga of Moses (Ex. 2; cf. Josephus, *Antt.* II, 205–23) and in many Greek and Roman authors (cf. the extensive survey in Luz 1992: 84), and is often associated with that of an infanticide. Cf. also Suetonius, *Augustus* 94:

'According to Julius Marathus, a few months before August was born a portent was generally observed at Rome, which gave warning that nature was pregnant with a king for the Roman people; thereupon the senate in consternation decreed that no male child born that year should be reared; but those whose wives were with child saw to it that the decree was not filed in the treasury (i.e. did not assume the force of law).'

History

The exegesis which has been carried out and which indicated a redactional shaping throughout, along with the observations at the beginning (see 'General' above) and the parallel motifs mentioned, shows that the historical content of Matt. 2 is nil.

Similarly, the fact that Luke as well as Matthew has a birth narrative does not contribute anything to the historical credibility of Matthew's narrative. On the contrary, because the two accounts are incompatible their historical value is even less.

- Matthew and Luke do not agree once in dating the birth of Jesus. In Matthew the birth of Jesus is said to have taken place while Herod the Great was still alive (he died in 4 BCE); by contrast, in Luke Jesus was born shortly after a tax assessment ordered by the emperor Augustus at the time when Quirinius was governor of Syria (from 6 CE). However, we know nothing from non-Christian sources of a census under Augustus which extended throughout the empire. The first census in Judaea (not in the whole of the Roman empire) was only made in 6/7 CE.
- In Matthew, Jesus' parents live in Bethlehem and move to Nazareth only after the return from Egypt. By contrast, Luke has the parents go to Bethlehem from their abode in Nazareth before the birth of Jesus.
- Luke reports nothing about magicians from the East, a miraculous star, a flight to Egypt and an infanticide by

Herod; conversely, Matthew knows nothing of a proclamation of Jesus' birth to the shepherds.

A last attempt, as desperate as it is misplaced, to harmonize the two narratives would be to assume that both sought to depict the same thing in different ways or that what was reported by Matthew presupposed the Lukan account of what had happened previously (or vice versa). Rather:

'As we have before us two equally unhistorical narratives, there is no reason for preferring a forced and unnatural derivation of Matthew's narrative from that of Luke, to the very simple derivation which may be traced through Old Testament passages and Jewish notions. These two descriptions of the introduction of Jesus into the world, are, therefore, two variations on the same theme, composed, however, quite independently of each other' (Strauss 1972: 178)

A curious example of how presumptuous those who want to maintain the historicity of biblical stories at any price can be is offered by Werner Keller's book *The Bible as History*. Keller reconstructs the events which he supposes to have preceded those reported in the story of the magicians as follows: three Jews studying astrology in Babylonia had interpreted the star of Bethlehem, in reality a conjunction of Saturn and Jupiter in the sign of Pisces, in terms of the appearance of a mighty king in the West, the land of their fathers:

'On May 29th in the year 7 BC they observed the first encounter of the two planets from the roof of the School of Astrology at Sippar. At that time of year the heat was already unbearable in Mesopotamia. Summer is no time for long and difficult journeys. Besides that, they knew about the second conjunction on October 3rd. They could predict this encounter in advance as accurately as future eclipses of the sun and moon. The fact that October 3rd was the Jewish Day of Atonement may have been taken as

87

a warning, and at that point they may have started out on their journey (1957: 333).

The Jewish astrologers are said to have arrived in Jerusalem on their camels towards the end of November and history took its well-known course.

We are justified in firmly rejecting these and other off-beat speculations (cf. in a model way Smend 1997: 41–5). But that makes it seem all the more necessary to require an explanation from Smend himself who, in the end, contrary to all the historical facts, joins the Bible in saying: 'God led Israel out of Egypt and Jesus Christ is risen from the dead' (ibid., 45). For what sense do such lofty statements make if they have been refuted historically once and for all?

Matt. 12.46–50
Jesus' true kinsfolk

> '46 While he was still speaking to the people, *behold*, his mother and his brothers stood outside, asking to speak to him. 47 *Someone* told him, "Your mother and your brothers are standing outside, asking to speak to you." 48 But he replied *to the one who told him*, "Who is my mother, and who are my brothers?" 49 And he *stretched out his hand over his disciples* and said, "Here are my mother and my brothers! 50 For whoever does the will of my Father in heaven is my brother, and sister, and mother."'

Redaction

The author's intention can be discovered from a comparison of the present narrative with Mark 3.31–35, on which it is based. Matthew's text (like the parallel in Luke) is rather more friendly to the family by comparison with the harsh repudiation depicted in Mark. This is toned down in two ways: *first*, Matthew (like Luke) simply omits the text of

Mark 3.20f. – and thus the assumption of Jesus' kinsfolk that he is out of his mind. *Secondly*, he abbreviates the report of the arrival of Jesus' kinsfolk. These are now no longer separated from Jesus by the crowd which surrounds him (Mark 3.32a). In keeping with this,

[47f.] Not the crowd, but an unnamed person announces the arrival of the relatives and is spoken to by Jesus.

[49] Jesus' gesture emphasizes his devotion to the disciples. They are the ones whom Jesus identifies with his mother and his brothers.

[50] In contrast to Mark 3.35 ('God'), this verse speaks of 'my Father in heaven' in a way typical of the First Evangelist.

Matt. 13.54–58
The rejection of Jesus in his ancestral city

'53 And he came into his ancestral city and taught them in *their* synagogue, so that they were astonished, and said, "Where did this man get this wisdom and these mighty works? 55 Is not this the *craftsman's son*? *Is not his mother called Mary?* And are not his brothers James and *Joseph* and Simon and Judas? 56 And are not all his sisters with us? Where then did this man get all this?"

57 And they took offence at him. But Jesus said to them, "A prophet is not without honour except in his ancestral city and in his own house." 58 And he did not do many mighty works there, because of their unbelief.'

Redaction

The intention of this text can be discovered from a comparison with Mark 6.1–6, on which it is based.

[54] By comparison with Mark 6.1f. this verse displays three changes. First, the disciples are not mentioned; secondly, Jesus teaches in 'their' synagogue; thirdly, the miracles are not defined more closely (Mark 6.2: 'are wrought by his hands').

[55f.] By comparison with Mark 6.3 Jesus is not called 'craftsman' and 'son of Mary' but 'son of the craftsman'. In other words, Matthew suppresses the tradition of Jewish contemporaries which is critical of Jesus and which rightly contains a reference to his illegitimate birth. As in the Markan original, the extended listing of members of the family, which varies slightly from Mark 6.3, illustrates the interest of the neighbours: Jesus cannot be powerful and wise because his family is generally known.

[57] Matthew deletes the kinsfolk from the series of three in Mark 6.4.

[58] Matthew abbreviates the conclusion in Mark 6.5f. by omitting both the possibly offensive statement 'he could do no miracles there' and the remark that Jesus marvelled.

The Gospel of Luke and the Acts of the Apostles

General remarks on Luke 1.5–2.52

Preliminary comment: it should be noted that the infancy narratives of Luke 1–2 do not appear in Marcion, who compiled a Bible – consisting of the Gospel of Luke and seven letters of Paul – before the middle of the second century (cf. Lüdemann 1996: 164–6). Some exegetes, too, also argue that the infancy narratives were added to the Gospel of Luke only at a later stage. However, I assume that they were originally part of the Gospel.

In what follows, some texts will be discussed in a rather different order from that of the New Testament. This procedure already presupposes the source-critical result of the textual analyses which follow. The reason for this is as follows: the narratives about the announcement to Zechariah and the birth and naming of John the Baptist (Luke 1.5–25, 57–66) were originally one narrative handed down in isolation which was first torn apart by Luke's redactional activity. This emerges from the fact that v.57 joins on smoothly to v.25 and the story presupposes neither the announcement of the birth of Jesus (1.26–38) nor Mary's visit to Elizabeth (1.39–56). Conversely, however, the stories about Jesus go beyond the narrative about John the Baptist (cf. especially Luke 1.39–45) and the virgin birth, which is predicated only of Jesus.

In addition, the evangelist had two psalms (1.46–55* and 1.68–79*) and four quite independent traditions about the birth and childhood of Jesus, each in isolation. (The asterisk denotes the versions of the psalms in the tradition; Luke made additions to them and so their extents are no longer the same.)

Luke made the narrative about John parallel to the corresponding stories about Jesus, using a stylistic form known at the time, and linked it by the story of the encounter of the two mothers in Luke 1.39–45 (46–55), 56.

Original continuous tradition about John the Baptist	*Redactional link*	*Originally independent Jesus traditions*
1.5–25: Announcement of the birth of John the Baptist		1.26–38: Announcement of the birth of Jesus
	1.39–56: Visit of Mary to Elizabeth (46–55: Mary's song of praise)	
1.57–80: The birth and naming of John the Baptist (67–79: Zechariah's song of praise)		2.1–21: The birth of Jesus
		2.22–41: Presentation of Jesus in the temple
		2.42–52: The twelve-year-old Jesus in the temple

The analogous contrast between Philip and Simon (Magus) in Acts 8.4–13, which certainly comes from Luke (cf. Lüdemann 1989: 95f.), also supports the assumption that Luke himself shaped the parallel composition and did not already find the infancy narratives in parallel form.

Luke 1.5–25
The announcement of the birth of John the Baptist

'5 *In the days of Herod, king of Judaea,* there was a priest named Zechariah of the division of Abijah; and he had a wife from the daughters of Aaron, and her name was Elizabeth. 6 And they were both righteous before God, walking in all the commandments and ordinances of the Lord blameless. 7 But they had no child, because Elizabeth was barren, and both were already advanced in years.

8 Now while he was serving as priest before God when his division was on duty, 9 according to the custom of the priestly ministry it fell to him by lot to offer the incense offering. And he went into the the temple of the Lord. 10 *And the whole multitude of the people were praying outside at the hour of the incense offering.* 11 And there appeared to him an angel of the Lord, standing on the right side of the altar of incense. 12 And Zechariah was troubled when he saw him, and fear fell upon him. 13 But the angel said to him,

"Do not be afraid, Zechariah,
for your prayer has been heard,
and your wife Elizabeth will bear you a son,
and you shall call his name John.
14 And you will have joy and gladness,
and many will rejoice at his birth.
15 For he will become great before the Lord,
and he shall drink no wine nor strong drink,
and he will be filled with holy spirit,
even from his mother's womb.

16 And he will turn many of the sons of Israel
to the Lord their God.
17 And he will go before him
in the spirit and power of Elijah,
to turn the hearts of the fathers to the children,
and the disobedient to the wisdom of the just,
to make ready for the Lord a people prepared."
18 And Zechariah said to the angel, "How shall I know
this? For I am an old man, and my wife is advanced in
years."
19 And the angel answered him, "I am Gabriel, who stand
in the presence of God; and I was sent to speak to you, and
to bring you this good news. 20 And behold, you will be
dumb and unable to speak until the day that these things
come to pass, because you did not believe my words,
which will be fulfilled in their time."
21 *And the people were waiting for Zechariah, wondering
why he was spending so long in the temple.* 22 And when
he came out, he could not speak to them, and they perceived that he had seen a vision in the temple; and he made
signs to them and remained dumb.

23 And when his time of service was ended, he went to
his home. 24 After these days his wife Elizabeth conceived,
and for five months she hid herself, saying, 25 *"Thus the
Lord has done to me in the days when he looked on me,
to take away my shame."'*

Redaction

[5a] 'In the days... Judaea', the linking of the following narrative to Herod (the Great) corresponds to a concern we often
find in Luke to anchor dates of salvation history in secular
history. Later he will date the birth of Jesus to the time of the
emperor Augustus and the governorship of Quirinius (2.1f.)
and the appearance of John the Baptist to the fifteenth year
of the reign of the emperor Tiberius (3.1).

[5b–7] These verses form the exposition: Zechariah and

Elizabeth, both of priestly origin and morally blameless, have no children. Elizabeth's barrenness and the great age of the couple heighten the magnitude and the unusual and miraculous character of the event which will be reported next.

[8f.] An introduction to the decisive scene: by lot, Zechariah is one day given the task of offering incense in the temple.

[10] This goes back to Luke in its entirety. He adds the *motif of prayer* to the traditions at decisive points in the story of individuals and groups. Here are two examples: (a) at the baptism of Jesus by John, the Son of God prays (Luke 3.21); Mark 1.9–11, on which this is based, does not contain the features. (b) In Acts Luke makes the community prayer in 4.24–30 follow the scene before the supreme council (Acts 4.1–22), thus creating an impressive scenario: the young community has a strong God on its side who preserves it from its enemies despite all resistance.

[11f.] Zechariah's fear at the appearance of the angel is the typical human reaction to contact with the divine.

[13–17] The formula 'Do no be afraid' as an introduction to the angel's speech is equally a matter of style. The speech is divided into three parts. Verses 13–14 refer to the imminent future: to Zechariah is promised a son whose name is pre-destined by God. Verse 15 says that John will already be a prophet from his mother's womb, so that he needs no special calling. Verses 16–17 mention the future success of his activity: he will go before God or the Lord (here Luke is certainly thinking of the Messiah Jesus) to prepare a people who are equipped for him.

[18] Because of his great age and that of his wife (v.7) Zechariah asks for a sign to confirm the promise.

[19f.] The angel responds to the request for a sign by giving his name: he is Gabriel, one of the archangels (cf. Dan.8.16f.; 9.21). This indicates that the message comes directly from God and needs no confirmation by a sign. Therefore the sign which Zechariah is nevertheless given is at the same time punishment for his unbelief: he is to remain dumb until the birth of his son.

[21] That this is a redactional addition emerges not only from favourite Lukan words ('people', 'wait'), but above all from the fact that the phrase 'and the people were waiting' recurs almost word for word in Luke 3.15 and that here as in v.10 the focus is on the people before the temple.

[22] The 'punitive sign' announced in v.20 has already taken place when Zechariah leaves the temple. Instead of giving the blessing that the people expect, he can only nod.

[23–24a] But the promise also begins to be fulfilled immediately: as soon as Zechariah has returned home, Elizabeth's pregnancy begins.

[24b] This serves to link the story of John with that of Jesus and is redactional: 1.26 ('in the sixth month') refers to the five months.

[25] A redactional conclusion to the story. Elizabeth thanks God for removing the shame associated with her barrenness. Compare the Old Testament example of Hannah, whose childlessness is her humiliation (I Sam. 1.2) or her misery (I Sam. 1.11), but whose pregnancy is understood as her exaltation and as a humiliation of the enemies who had mocked her because of her barrenness (I Sam. 2.1).

Conclusion: Luke has taken up an existing narrative, added some features which slow down the action (vv.10 and 21), and only intervened more markedly at the end, in order to make the link with the story of Jesus.

Tradition and history

Cf. the summary remarks on the next section (1.57–66), which formed a unity with 1.5–25 at a pre-redactional level (cf. also above, pp. 90f.).

Luke 1.57–66
The birth of John the Baptist

'57 Now the time came for Elizabeth to be delivered, and

she gave birth to a son. 58 And her neighbours and kins-folk heard that the Lord had shown great mercy to her, and they rejoiced with her.

59 And on the eighth day they came to circumcise the child; and they wanted to name him Zechariah after his father. 60 But his mother said, "No, he shall be called John." 61 And they said to her, "None of your kinsfolk is called by this name." 62 And they made signs to his father, enquiring what he wanted him to be called. 63 And he asked for a writing tablet, and wrote, "His name is John." And they all marvelled. 64 And immediately his mouth was opened and his tongue loosed, and he spoke, praising God.

65 And fear came on all their neighbours. And all these things were talked about through all the hill country of Judaea 66 and all who heard them *laid them up in their hearts*, saying, "What will become of this child?" *And the hand of the Lord was with him.'*

Redaction

After the interruption by 1.26–38 and 1.39–56 this section resumes the narrative thread of 1.5–25:

[57f.] First the fulfilment of the message which had been given to Zechariah by the angel (1.13d) is reported.

[59–63] Then there is a description of the naming of the child commanded by the angel (1.13e).

[64] This refers back to 1.20: as the last day of Zechariah's dumbness has come, he is now given his voice back.

[65–66] These verses round off the story; the motif of the heart corresponds to Luke 2.19 and 2.51b, and the con-cluding remark to Luke 2.40.

Tradition

Luke may have had before him the story of the prophecy of the birth of John the Baptist and its fulfilment; here redaction and tradition cannot always be separated clearly. Both parts of the narrative 'hang together and form a real personal legend which depicts the significance of its hero by the events of his conception and birth' (Dibelius 1953: 3).

The original purpose of this legend was to depict John as a 'great man' who, chosen by God and coming from a priestly family, has the task of converting the people of Israel and preparing them for the coming of God himself.

That John is a forerunner and is inferior to Jesus, which it is vital for Christians to emphasize, indeed which is what makes the story of John the Baptist worth telling for Christians at all, does not feature at all here. For this reason the legend can hardly be of Christian origin. Rather, it is a tradition from circles around John the Baptist.

The *motifs* of the legend come from the Old Testament throughout:

(a) barrenness and/or old age as reasons for having no children,

(b) promise of a child by God or an angel and

(c) predetermination of the name by God.

These three motifs are also combined in Gen. 17.17–19. At God's announcement that Sarah would bear a son,

'17 Abraham fell on his face and laughed, and said to himself, "Shall a child be born to a man who is a hundred years old? Shall Sarah, who is ninety years old, bear a child?" 18 And Abraham said to God, "O that Ishmael might live in your sight!" 19 God said, "No, but Sarah your wife shall bear you a son, and you shall call his name Isaac . . ."'

The announcement of the birth of Samson in Judg. 13.2–5 displays a combination of the first two motifs mentioned; in general it is very similar to the beginning of the story of John together with the promise by the angel:

'2 And there was a certain man of Zorah, of the tribe of

97

the Danites, whose name was Manoah; and his wife was barren and had no children. 3 And the angel of the Lord appeared to the woman and said to her, "Behold, you are barren and have no children; but you shall conceive and bear a son. 4 Therefore beware, and drink no wine or strong drink, and eat nothing unclean, 5 for lo, you shall conceive and bear a son. No razor shall come upon his head, for the boy shall be a Nazirite to God from birth; and he shall begin to deliver Israel from the hand of the Philistines."'

For the individual motifs (a), (b) and (c), see further Gen.16.1f.,11; 18.10–15; I Sam. 1.

(d) The servants of God in Isaiah and Jeremiah are already called before their births:

'Listen to me, you islands, and hearken, you peoples from afar! The Lord called me from the womb, from the body of my mother he named me' (Isa.49.1).
'Before I formed you in the womb I knew you, and before you were born I consecrated you; I appointed you a prophet to the nations' (Jer.1.5).

(e) Abraham (Gen.15.8), Gideon (Judg. 6.36–40) and Hezekiah (II Kings 20.8f.) ask for signs.

History

The legendary and edifying character of the story together with the motifs which throughout have Old Testament parallels shows that the tradition underlying 1.5–25, 57–66 is unhistorical. Only the proper names derive from historical personalities.

Luke 1.67–80
Zechariah's hymn of praise ('Benedictus')

'67 *And his father Zechariah was filled with holy spirit,*

98

and prophesied, saying:
"68 Blessed be the Lord, the God of Israel,
for he has visited (his people) and brought liberation to
his people,
69 and raised up a horn of salvation for us
in the house of David, his servant,
70 *as always he spoke by the mouth of his holy
prophets,*
71 deliverance from our enemies, and from the hand of
all who hate us;
72 to show mercy to our fathers,
and to remember his holy covenant,
73 the oath which he swore to Abraham, our father,
to grant us 74 without fear, delivered from the hand of
enemies,
to serve him 75 in holiness and righteousness
before him all our days.
76 *And you, child, will be called the prophet of the
Most High;*
for you will go before the Lord to prepare his ways,
77 *to give knowledge of deliverance to his people*
in forgiveness of their sins,
78 *through the tender mercy of our God,*
with which the dawn will visit us from on high
79 *to give light to those who sit in darkness and in the*
shadow of death,
to guide our feet into the way of peace."
80 *And the child grew and became strong in spirit, and he*
was in the wilderness till the day of his manifestation to
Israel.'

Redaction

Zechariah's song of praise, for which the name 'Benedictus',
the first word of the Latin translation, has become established, follows when the story of John the Baptist's birth is
already complete. This position makes it clear that the song

is not part of the original personal legend, in which it would have had an appropriate place after v.64. Rather, it was added at the end of the previous narrative only at a later stage, probably by Luke.

Within the section 1.67–80 the following elements are to be attributed to Luke's redaction.

[67] This is Lukan in language and is a redactional transitional verse.

[70] This verse corresponds almost word for word with Acts 3.21b. It is the only real subsidiary clause within the song and for that reason too may derive from Luke.

[76–77] Verse 76a forms a counterpart to 1.32. Verses 76b–77 may also be a Lukan insertion. This emphasizes the role of John as forerunner – a motif which will be developed later: cf. Luke 3.2–6 (using Mark 1.2) and 7.26f. John's message, 'to give knowledge of deliverance to his people in forgiveness of their sins', anticipates Luke 3.3. 'Deliverance' does not appear in Mark and Matthew; it appears once in John (4.22), three times in the Lukan infancy narratives (1.69, 71, 77) and six times in Acts (4.12; 7.25; 13.26,47; 16.17; 27.34).

[80] This verse bridges the period up to John's public appearance in ch.3 and corresponds to Luke 2.40,52. Luke describes the growth and flourishing of the child in a stereotyped way. In Acts he will later depict the successful dissemination of the word of God and the constant growth of the church in a similar way (Acts 1.15: around 120 believers; 2.41: 3,000).

Conclusion: Luke took up an already existing psalm and supplemented it for his purposes by emphasizing the role of John as forerunner.

Tradition

The original messianic hymn is of Jewish origin. As in Mary's hymn (1.46–55), there are numerous Old Testament parallel phrases for each verse (cf. the commentaries).

Zechariah never spoke the hymn attributed to him.

Luke 1.26–38
The announcement of the birth of Jesus

'1.26 In the sixth month the angel Gabriel was sent from God to a city of Galilee named Nazareth, 27 to a virgin *betrothed to a man whose name was Joseph* of the house of David; and the virgin's name was Mary.

28 And he came to her and said, "Hail, O favoured one, the Lord is with you!"

29 But she was greatly troubled at the saying, and considered in her mind what this greeting meant.

30 And the angel said to her,
"Do not be afraid, Mary,
for you have found favour with God.

31 And behold, you will become pregnant
and bear a son,
and you shall call his name Jesus.

32 He will be great,
and will be called the Son of the Most High,
and God the Lord will give him the throne of David his father,

33 and he will be king over the house of Jacob for ever;
and of his kingdom there will be no end."

34 And Mary said to the angel, "How shall this be, since I know no man?"

35 And the angel answered and said to her,
"Holy spirit will come upon
and power of the Most High will overshadow you;
therefore the holy thing to be born
will be called the Son of God.

36 *And behold, your kinswoman Elizabeth in her old age has also conceived a son; and this is the sixth month for her who was called barren. 37 For with God nothing is impossible."*

38 Mary said, "Behold the Lord's slave; let it be to me as you have said."
And the angel departed from her.'

Redaction

[26] The date ('in the sixth month') refers to the note in 1.24 that Elizabeth hid herself for five months and forms a redactional link between the two stories. The angel Gabriel is known from 1.5–25. Nazareth in Galilee is a possible historical reminiscence of the birthplace of Jesus. But because according to the Old Testament prophecy in Micah 5.1f. the Messiah 'had to' come from Bethlehem (see pp. 112f. below), Luke has the parents of Jesus travel there later (2.1ff.).

[27] This verse introduces Mary and Joseph; Mary is presented in a very circuitous way as Joseph's betrothed.

[28f.] The scene corresponds to 1.11f.: Zechariah is shaken and Mary is overwhelmed.

[30–33] The two five-line strophes containing the words of the angel are not Luke's style anywhere.

[34f.] Mary's question is hard to reconcile with v.27: a fiancée can hardly be surprised at the promise of a child even if she has as yet had no sexual intercourse with her fiancé. Therefore it has been conjectured that vv.34–35 are a secondary Lukan addition which inserts the notion of the virgin birth into the original story (Bultmann 1968: 295). However, the fact that in the following stories, which are about the fulfilment of the promise (with the exception of 2.21), Luke makes no connection with the scene in which the promise is made and in particular does not mention the virginal conception either in the Gospel or Acts, tells against this (cf. Dibelius 1953: 9–16).

It is therefore more probable that it is not the virgin birth but *Joseph* who has been inserted into the narrative at a secondary stage in v.27, especially as he plays no further role at all in the following story, which is focussed wholly on Mary.

[36f.] These verses, which refer back to 1.24,26, are redactional and serve to link the two narrative strands.

[38] This outdoes the announcement to Zechariah. Whereas Zechariah has to keep silent, Mary accedes to the angel's will.

Conclusion: Luke has inserted a story about the annunciation to Mary which he had into the story of John, linked it with that story through vv.26, 36f., and inserted Joseph (v.27). That in so doing he took into account the manifest contradiction between v.27 and v.34 may be explained by the fact that he imagined that the conception took place at the moment of the annunciation, or more precisely that what was announced took place when Mary declared herself ready ('Let it be to me as you have said').

By making the story parallel with the story of the announcement of the birth of John the Baptist to Zechariah, Luke at the same time outdoes that story with the motif of the virginal conception.

Tradition

The legend probably derives from Jewish-Hellenistic circles which wanted to maintain the procreation by the spirit, the true sonship of the Messiah and the virgin birth in the same story (see above, pp. 72–6).

The structural parallels to the story of the announcement of the birth of John can be explained from the fact that the two narratives follow the pattern of Old Testament announcements of births (cf. above, pp. 97 f.).

History

That the story in the tradition is legendary throughout shows it to be unhistorical.

Mary's visit to Elizabeth

'39 *In those days Mary arose and went with haste into the hill country, to a city in Judah, 40 and she entered the house of Zechariah and greeted Elizabeth. 41 And when Elizabeth heard the greeting of Mary, the child leaped in her womb; and Elizabeth was filled with holy spirit 42 and she cried with a loud voice, "Blessed are you among women, and blessed is the fruit of your womb! 43 And how does it happen that the mother of the Lord should come to me? 44 For behold, when the voice of your greeting came to my ears, the child in my body leaped for joy. 45 And blessed are you to have believed. For what has been said to you by the Lord will be fulfilled."'*

Redaction

[39f.] Mary's visit to Elizabeth is motivated by the reference of the angel in 1.36. 'Hill country' is taken over from 1.65.

[41a] The leaping of the child in the womb emphasizes the inferiority of John the Baptist: even before John is born he exercises his 'function as prophetic forerunner' (Bovon 1989: 85). Probably Luke 1.15 influenced the formulation of this verse.

[41b] This corresponds word for word to the redactional verse 1.67.

[42] By the beatitude Elizabeth subordinates herself to Mary and her still unborn child.

[43] No answer is given to Elizabeth's question, nor is one expected. Rather, 'How does it happen?' again emphasizes the superiority of Mary and thus her child to John the Baptist and his mother.

[44] This repeats v.41a in the first person singular, largely word for word.

[45] A reference to the prophecy of the angel and Mary's reaction in 1.26–38. However, Elizabeth cannot know of this

any more than of Mary's pregnancy (v.42). Luke probably imagined that she nevertheless mentions it because she speaks as one filled with the Holy Spirit.

Conclusion: the section serves as a link between the passages about John the Baptist and those about Jesus and at the same time emphasizes Jesus' superiority to John the Baptist. It is redactional throughout and has no historical background.

Luke 1.46–56
Mary's song of praise ('Magnificat')

'46 *And Mary said:*
"My soul magnifies the Lord,
47 and my spirit rejoices in God my Saviour,
48 for he has regarded the lowliness of his slave.
For behold, from now on all children's children will call me blessed.
49 For the mighty one has done great things for me,
and holy is his name.
50 And his mercy lasts from generation to generation
among those who fear him.
51 He shows strength with his arm
and scatters those who are proud in the imagination of their hearts.
52 He casts down the mighty from their thrones,
and exalts the lowly.
53 He fills the hungry with good things,
and the rich he sends empty away.
54 He has accepted Israel, his servant,
in remembrance of his mercy,
55 as he spoke to our fathers,
to Abraham and to his posterity for ever."
56 And Mary remained with her about three months; after that she returned to her home.'

[46a] Several Latin manuscripts have the name Elizabeth instead of Mary. But according to *Luke* it is beyond doubt

Mary who utters the hymn. Nevertheless – regardless of textual criticism – the question arises whether at the pre-redactional stage the hymn was handed down as a hymn of Elizabeth (see below).

[46b–55] The hymn, which is usually called 'Magnificat' ('It exalts') after the first word of the Latin translation in v.46b, has been inserted into the story of Mary's visit to Elizabeth (cf. similarly Ex. 15.1–18; Num. 23f.; Deut. 32; Judg. 5, etc.) and cannot be recognized with certainty in either language or content as a redactional intervention. The only exception is v.48b, which provides the reference to the situation and moreover shows a change of subject from God to the children's children (for v.48a see below).

[56] This is the redactional conclusion to the story of Mary's visit to Elizabeth. The 'three months', together with 1.26, make nine months in all and form a transition to the subsequent story of the birth of John the Baptist.

Conclusion: Luke has taken a pre-existing psalm and put it in Mary's mouth in the framework of the scene which he has created of the encounter of the two expectant mothers (1.39–45,56). He does so in order to make Elizabeth even more clearly subordinate to Mary and to legitimate the high esteem there is for Mary (v.48b). It has been argued that Luke composed the psalm in the style of the Septuagint. However, not only v.48b but also the fact that on such a presupposition clearer references to the context would be expected (there is no mention at all of a pregnancy or birth) tell against the thesis.

Tradition

The first part of the hymn in the tradition has features of an individual song of thanksgiving (vv.46b–49). The second (vv.50–53) describes God's action towards human beings in general; here vv.52ab/53ab have a chiastic formulation (A–B–B–A). The third describes God's special concern for Israel (vv.54f.).

Numerous Old Testament parallel phrases can be demonstrated for each individual verse (cf. the commentaries); however, the song of the formerly barren Hannah after the birth of Samuel (I Sam. 2.1–10), which the author doubtless knew, clearly had the most influence:

'1 And Hannah prayed and said:
"My heart exults in the Lord
my head is exalted in the Lord.
My mouth has opened wide against my enemies,
because I rejoice in your salvation.
2 There is no one holy like the Lord, there is no one like you,
there is no rock like our God.
3 Talk no more so very proudly,
let not arrogance come from your mouth;
for the Lord is a God who notices things
and by him actions are weighed.
4. The bow of the mighty is shattered,
but the feeble is girded with strength.
5 Those who were full have to serve for bread
but those who were hungry have ceased to hunger.
The barren has borne seven
but she who has many children is forlorn.
6 The Lord kills and makes alive,
he brings down to Sheol and raises up.
The Lord makes poor and makes rich;
he humbles and exalts.
8 He raises up the needy from the dust,
he makes them sit with princes
and inherit a seat of honour.
For the foundations of the earth are the Lord's,
and on them he has set the world.
9 He will protect the feet of his faithful ones;
but the wicked shall be cut off in darkness
for much might helps no one.
10 Those who quarrel with the Lord shall perish;

against them he will thunder in heaven;
the Lord will judge the ends of the earth.
He will give power to his king,
and exalt the head of his anointed."'

The similarity of Luke 1.46–55 to this song is a strong argument for the assumption that the Magnificat was originally
handed down as a hymn of Elizabeth. For – in contrast to
Mary – like Hannah, Elizabeth was barren for a long time.
This assumption is further supported by the vow of the still
childless Hannah in I Sam. 1.11, which recalls v.48a: 'Lord
Sabaoth, if you will look on the affliction of your slave . . .
and give your slave a son, I will give him to the Lord all the
days of his life . . .'

If, however, we were to assume that the psalm in the
tradition had originally been independent of Elizabeth, we
would probably also have to attribute v.48a to Luke, who
would then have taken over Mary's designation of herself as
'slave' from Luke 1.38 and understood the 'lowliness' not as
the shame of barrenness but as a humble attitude.

History

The Magnificat may or may not originally have been handed
down as a psalm of Elizabeth, but neither she nor Mary ever
spoke the psalm. That already emerges from the fact that the
scenic framework in which it is meant to be spoken is pure
fiction.

David Friedrich Strauss already remarked on the historical
question that it cannot be 'thought natural that two friends
visiting each other should, even in the midst of the most
extraordinary occurrences, break forth into long hymns, and
in their conversation should entirely lose the character of
dialogue'. But if the hymn is to be understood as the work of
the Holy Spirit, 'it is surprising that a speech emanating
immediately from the divine source of inspiration should
not be more striking for its originality, but should be so

interlarded with reminiscences from the Old Testament, borrowed from the song of praise spoken by the mother of Samuel in analogous circumstances' (1972: 150).

Luke 2.1–21
The birth of Jesus

'1 *In those days a decree went out from Caesar Augustus that all the world should be assessed. 2 This was the first assessment, when Quirinius was governor of Syria. 3 And all went to be asssessed, each to his own city. 4 And Joseph also went up from Galilee, from the city of Nazareth, to Judaea, to the city of David, which is called Bethlehem, because he was of the house and lineage of David, 5 to be enrolled with Mary his betrothed, who was pregnant.*

6 And *while they were there*, the time came for her to be delivered. 7 And she gave birth to her first-born son and wrapped him in swaddling cloths, and laid him in a manger, because there was no place for them in the inn.

8 And in that region there were shepherds out in the field, keeping watch over their flock by night. 9 And the angel of the Lord came to them and the glory of the Lord shone around them, and they were very frightened.

10 And the angel said to them, "Do not be afraid; for behold, I bring you good news of a great joy which all the people will share; 11 for to you is born today in the city of David a Saviour, *who is Christ the Lord*. 12 And this (shall be) a sign for you: you will find a child wrapped in swaddling cloths and lying in a manger."

13 And suddenly there was with the angel the multitude of the heavenly hosts praising God and saying, 14 "Glory to God in the highest, and on earth peace among men with whom he is pleased!"

15 When the angels had gone away from them into heaven, the shepherds said to one another, "Let us now go to Bethlehem and see the story that has happened, which the Lord has made known to us." 16 And they went with

haste, and found both Mary and Joseph, and the baby lying in a manger. 17 And when they had seen it, they made known the saying which had been told them about this child. 18 And all who heard it wondered at what the shepherds told them. *19 But Mary kept all these sayings and pondered them in her heart.* 20 And the shepherds returned, glorifying and praising God for all they had heard and seen, as it had been told them.

21 And at the end of eight days, when the child had to be circumcised, he was called Jesus, the name given to him by the angel before he was conceived in the womb.'

Redaction

[1–5] With the motif of the census Luke puts the story of Jesus' birth in the context of world history (cf. above p. 93 on Luke 1.5). Moreover, Joseph's journey to his home town makes it possible for Luke to take account in the narrative of the requirement of salvation history for the Messiah to be born in Bethlehem (cf. Micah 5.1f.).

In describing Mary as Joseph's betrothed, Luke makes a connection between this story and 1.26–38 (see below). Given the context, however, Mary must already be Joseph's wife. For as his fiancée she would still count as being in her father's house and neither could have gone nor have been allowed to go with Joseph.

[6–7a] The information 'while they were there' refers to Bethlehem (v.4) and therefore similarly derives from Luke. In the birth, which is reported briefly, the prophecy from 1.26–38 is fulfilled without explicit reference being made to it.

[7b] The statement 'and laid him . . . no place' follows abruptly. Previously there had been no mention of an inn.

[8] This verse brings a change of scene and introduces a self-contained narrative of the proclamation of the birth to the shepherds.

[9] In typical fashion there is a report of the appearance of an

angel with shining light and of the reaction of the shepherds.
[10–12] The formula 'Do not be afraid' with which the angel
introduces his words (cf. also Luke 1.11–13) is equally
typical. By comparison with the message of the angel in
1.32f. the christological focal point in v.11 is different: if
there the royal function of the child is developed, here the
emphasis lies on Jesus' soteriological function ('saviour') – an
indication of the independence of the traditions which under-
lie the two passages (see below). The manger as a sign points
back to v.7.

[13f.] The angel's message is supplemented with a hymn of
praise from the heavenly hosts.

[15–18] These verses report the shepherds' reaction to the
angel's message. As is announced in v.12, they find the child
in the manger.

[19] This verse corresponds to 2.51b and is redactional.
Doubtless Luke thinks that Mary was the source of his
narratives, at least the story of the announcement of Jesus'
birth. However, the assumption that in v.19 (and 2.51b) he
wanted to make an explicit reference to Mary as guarantor of
his tradition will not stand up, since elsewhere he does not
name his sources. Rather, here we have a sign of Luke's
special interest in the person of Mary herself. Verse 19 shows
her to be a quasi-believing Christian, as subsequently emerges
from an application of the parable of the sower: 'And as for
that in the good soil, they are those who, hearing the word,
hold it fast in a honest and good heart and bring forth fruit
with patience' (Luke 8.15).

[20] This verse rounds off the narrative with a choral conclusion.

[21] This verse is independent. It refers back to the story of
the annunciation and is a redactional construction analogous
to the story of John (cf. 1.59).

Conclusion: Luke has taken up a narrative about the
proclamation of the birth to the shepherds and given it a new
introduction (v.1–5). It is clear that at the pre-redactional
level this narrative cannot have been the continuation of the

story of the annunciation (1.26–38). For it makes no reference to a miraculous conception, and Mary evidently learns about the kind of child she has only through the visit of the shepherds. The difficulty in linking the two stories from the tradition lay in the fact that Joseph did not appear in the story of the annunciation, whereas the story of the shepherds was about an ordinary married couple. Luke has solved the problem by adding Joseph to the first story and making his wife Mary his fiancée in the second story.

Tradition

The basic material in vv.(6–7) 8–20 is an originally independent narrative, 'throughout a unitary narrative about the revelation of the birth of the Messiah to the shepherds' (Schneider 1977: 65). It is the story of a proclamation, the beginning of which has been overlaid with the redactional prefixing of the motif of the census; this beginning can no longer be reconstructed. Probably only fragments of it have been preserved in vv.6–7.

The sudden appearance of a great host of angels who join the one angel already present makes us ask whether vv.13–15a have not been added to the story in the course of the tradition.

The terms 'proclaim' (v.10) and 'saviour' (v.11) suggest that the legend originated in Hellenistic Christianity. The motif of the proclamation of the birth to the shepherds also points in this direction. For in Judaism shepherds were not regarded as being particularly pious: rather, their calling was almost despised (cf. the instances in Dibelius 1953: 64f.). By contrast, shepherds have a prominent place in oriental and above all Greek sagas. Here the shepherd exercises a calling which is well pleasing to God and recalls the primal time when gods still had dealings with human beings. In his contemplative existence the shepherd is particularly able to hear divine voices (cf. Dibelius 1953: 72f.).

The expectation that the Messiah will come from

Bethlehem, the home city of David (I Sam. 17.12–15; 20.6), is widespread in Judaism. Cf. Targum Micah 5.1:

> 'You Bethlehem – how small you were to be counted among the thousands of the house of Judah – from you will come forth through me the Messiah, to bear rule over Israel, whose name is named from the beginning, since the days of the world' (Billerbeck I, 83).

History

The historical yield of the Lukan infancy stories of the birth of Jesus is virtually nil (cf. above, p. 86, on Matt. 2.1–23). At the same time, Luke's statement that Jesus was Mary's first-born son (v.7) goes back to reliable information.

Luke 2.22–40
The presentation of Jesus in the temple; Simeon and Anna

> '22 *And when the time had come for their purification according to the law of Moses, they brought him up to Jerusalem to present him to the Lord,* 23 *as it is written in the law of the Lord,* "Every male that opens the womb shall be called holy to the Lord", 24 *and to offer a sacrifice according to what is said in the law of the Lord,* "a pair of turtledoves, or two young pigeons".
> 25 Now there was a man in Jerusalem whose name was Simeon, and this man was righteous and devout, and was waiting for the consolation of Israel, and the Holy Spirit was with him. 26 And it had been revealed to him by the Holy Spirit that he should not see death before he had seen the Lord's Christ. 27 And inspired by the Spirit he came into the temple; and when the parents brought in the child Jesus, to do for him according to the custom of the law, 28 he took him up in his arms and blessed God and said,
> 29 "Lord, now let your servant depart in peace, as you have said;

30 for my eyes have seen your salvation
31 which you have prepared before all peoples,
32 a light to lighten the Gentiles, and for the glory of your people Israel."
33 And his father and his mother marvelled at what was said about him. 34 And Simeon blessed them and said to Mary his mother, "Behold, this child is set for the fall and rising of many in Israel, and for a sign that will be spoken against 35 (*and a sword will pierce through your own soul also*), that thoughts out of many hearts may be revealed."
36 And there was a prophetess, Anna, the daughter of Phanuel, of the tribe of Asher; she was of a great age. She had lived with her husband seven years after she married, 37 and was now a widow of eighty-four. She did not depart from the temple, worshipping with fasting and prayer night and day. 38 She came up at that very hour and praised God, and spoke of him to all who were waiting for the redemption of Jerusalem.
39 *And when they had performed everything according to the law of the Lord, they returned into Galilee, to their city, Nazareth. 40 And the child grew and became strong, filled with wisdom; and the favour of God was upon him.*'

Redaction

[22–24] These verses introduce the two following scenes and serve to provide a reason for Jesus' presence in the temple. The ignorance of the precepts of the Jewish law shows that this introduction is redactional: the author thinks that both mother *and* child (or father?) have to be purified. In fact only the purification of the mother, thirty-three days after circumcision, was necessary (Lev. 12.2–8). By contrast there was no precept of the law which required the presentation of the firstborn in the temple.

Elsewhere, too, Luke is not very familiar with the Jewish law, as the two following examples show: (a) Acts 16.3 presupposes that the status of Timothy is determined by his

Greek father – and not, as was customary in Judaism with mixed marriages – through his Jewish mother (cf. Lüdemann 1989: 173–5). (b) Luke assumes that the Nazirate lasts seven days (Acts 21.27); in reality it lasted at least thirty days (cf. Billerbeck II, 80–8).

[25–28] These verses introduce Simeon. Living in an imminent expectation of the Messiah, he comes to the temple at the precise moment when Joseph and Mary bring in the child.

[29–32] With a prophetic song of praise (the so-called 'Nunc dimittis'), he praises God for the fulfilment of a revelation which concerns him personally (v.26) and for the universal salvation realized in Jesus, which also embraces the Gentile nations (in v.31 the word *laos* in the plural, which elsewhere is reserved for the people of God, denotes the Gentiles; v.32a differs: here *ethnos* denotes the people of God).

[33] Jesus' father and mother are amazed at Simeon's words – a reaction which is more than astonishing after 1.26ff. and 2.8ff.

It is interesting that some textual witnesses replace 'his father' by 'Joseph'. The underlying tendency here is to force Joseph's fatherhood into the background, as it was felt inappropriate in the context of the virgin birth.

[34–35] Simeon once again takes the initiative. He blesses the parents and addresses Mary directly. In speaking of the decision which Jesus will present to the people, to some extent he narrows the universal perspective of vv.31f. The saying about the sword (v.35a) is a somewhat clumsy insertion, probably by Luke: in the context of vv.34, 35b it suggests a clash between the mother and the son, but is meant to prophesy the mother's pain at the passion of Jesus.

[36–38] The second scene is a straight report on the prophetess Hannah, of whom 'all kinds of things are said . . . though she herself has nothing to say' (Dibelius 1961: 126).

[39] This verse, which rounds off the story, is similar to Luke 2.51a and refers back to v.22.

[40] This verse is redactional: cf. the parallels to John in Luke 1.66b, 80 and Luke 2.52.

Conclusion: Luke's redaction is visible only in the framework of the narrative and in the introduction of the motif of the mother's pain in v.35a.

Tradition

This story which Luke had might already have contained both the juxtaposition of Simeon's different prophecies in vv.29–32 and v.34f. and also the Anna scene, which was added at a secondary stage. Had Luke himself created or inserted one of the two Simeon sayings, it would be difficult to see why he did not put it on the lips of the 'speechless' prophetess.

It is certain that the Simeon legend was originally an independent story which presupposed neither the story of the annunciation nor the story of the shepherds. For Simeon's prophecy makes sense and impresses only if it is the first, and the amazement of the parents (v.33) can be expressed only if they had no idea beforehand that their child was destined to be the saviour (cf. Bultmann 1968: 300; Dibelius 1934: 127).

History

The story projects the post-Easter belief in Jesus on to his childhood. Its historical value is therefore nil.

Luke 2.41–52
The twelve-year-old Jesus in the temple

'41 Now his parents went to Jerusalem every year at the feast of the Passover. 42 And when he was twelve years old, they went up according to custom of the feast. 43 And when the days were ended and they were returning home, the boy Jesus stayed behind in Jerusalem, and his parents did not know it. 44 But supposing him to be in the company they went a day's journey, and they sought him among their kinsfolk and acquaintances.

45 And when they did not find him, they returned to Jerusalem, seeking him.

46 After three days they found him in the temple, sitting among the teachers, listening to them and asking them questions. 47 *And all who heard him were amazed at his understanding and his answers.*

48 And when they saw him they were astonished. And his mother said to him, "Son, why have you treated us so? Behold, your father and I have been looking for you anxiously."

49 And he said to them, "How is it that you sought me? Did you not know that I must be in that which is my Father's?"

50 And they did not understand the saying which he spoke to them. 51 *And he went down with them and came to Nazareth, and was obedient to them. And his mother kept all these things in her heart.*

52 *And Jesus increased in wisdom and in stature, and in favour with God and man.'*

Redaction

[41–45] These verses describe the situation. After the end of a pilgrimage the twelve-year-old Jesus, unnoticed by his parents, remains behind in Jerusalem. When his parents notice his absence, they return to look for him.

[46] This verse reports the success of their search: Joseph and Mary find Jesus among the teachers in the temple.

[47] Whereas in v.46 Jesus was the one who listened and asked questions, here it is presupposed that he also gives answers. This does not in itself prove the assumption that this is a redactional addition; however, that is confirmed by the fact that – apart from the Lukan vocabulary (cf. Acts 9.21) –

[48] the subject changes abruptly from the audience to the parents. The mother's question is followed by Jesus' answer.

[49] The point of the story, that as son of God Jesus belongs in his father's house, is made here. In the context of the Gospel of Luke these words – moreover the first reported to have been spoken by Jesus – probably envisage the procreation of Jesus by the Holy Spirit and the virgin birth (cf. later Luke 23.46).

[50] The parents react to their child's answer with incomprehension (cf.2.33). The sentence 'indicates the context in the life of Jesus and would be disruptive in a legend which moves towards a happy ending' (Dibelius 1934: 106). But if we assume that it is a Lukan addition, we would immediately have to assume that Luke did not sense the contradiction with v.51b, which is certainly redactional.

[51a] The 'record about the return to Nazareth is no necessary part of the legend' (Dibelius 1934: 106) and may therefore come from Luke (2.39).

[51b] This echoes 2.19 and certainly comes from Luke (for the contrast with v.50 see above). Similarly:

[52] This verse is redactional: the maturing of the child corresponds to 1.80 and 2.40 and to some degree bridges the period up to the baptism and the public appearance of the adult Jesus (3.21,23).

Conclusion: Luke has taken a self-contained story and put it in his own words. With the addition of v.47 he has attached as much importance to the unusual wisdom of the child as to the point of the traditional story in v.49b.

Tradition

The original independent story presupposes neither the miracle of the annunciation or the birth nor any knowledge of the parents that their child is the Messiah.

We may not claim an especially authoritative source for

this story. Verse 51 (like Mark 16.8) explains why the story came to be known only at a relatively late stage. Granted, both the women who discovered the empty tomb and Mary, who had heard the words of the twelve-year-old Jesus, kept silent for a long time. But in the light of the Easter event or the fulfilment of the promises they finally break their silence.

History

The episode is unhistorical. Martin Dibelius has thoroughly discussed the question of the historicity of such narratives in connection with this 'very beautiful example of a Jesus legend'. He writes:

> 'The figure of his hero is given to the narrator of such a personal legend: he regards it as historical, and does not reflect further on the possibility of its existence. The essential interest is not directed towards the greatness of a more or less miraculous fact . . . but to the edifying character of the whole . . . This dominant interest may, and in many cases does, lead to an unhistorical accentuation of the miraculous, to a glorifying of the hero and to a transfiguration of his life. Simple events are surrounded with a heavenly light, or elements from other legends are transferred to the hero in order to show the connection of his life with the divine world. But above all, his life is decorated with characters and scenes which correspond to the very nature of legendary biography' (1934: 108).

Luke 3.23–38
The genealogy of Jesus

> 23 And Jesus, when he began his ministry, was about thirty years of age, being the son (as was supposed) of Joseph,
> the son of Heli,
> 24 the son of Matthat,

119

the son of Levi,
the son of Melchi,
the son of Jannai,
the son of Joseph,
25 the son of Mattathias,
the son of Amos,
the son of Nahum,
the son of Esli,
the son of Naggai,
26 the son of Maath,
the son of Mattathias,
the son of Semein,
the son of Josech,
the son of Joda,
27 the son of Joanan,
the son of Rhesa,
the son of Zerubbabel,
the son of Shealtiel,
the son of Neri,
28 the son of Melchi,
the son of Addi,
the son of Cosam,
the son of Elmadam,
the son of Er,
29 the son of Joshua,
the son of Eliezer,
the son of Jorim,
the son of Matthat,
the son of Levi,
30 the son of Simeon,
the son of Judah,
the son of Joseph,
the son of Jonam,
the son of Eliakim,
31 the son of Melea,
the son of Menna,
the son of Mattatha,

the son of Nathan,
the son of David,
32 the son of Jesse,
the son of Obed,
the son of Boaz,
the son of Sala,
the son of Nahshon,
33 the son of Amminadab,
the son of Admin,
the son of Arni,
the son of Hezron,
the son of Perez,
the son of Judah,
34 the son of Jacob,
the son of Isaac,
the son of Abraham,
the son of Terah,
the son of Nahor,
35 the son of Serug,
the son of Reu,
the son of Peleg,
the son of Eber,
the son of Shelah,
36 the son of Cainan,
the son of Arphaxad,
the son of Shem,
the son of Noah,
the son of Lamech,
37 the son of Methuselah,
the son of Enoch,
the son of Jared,
the son of Mahalaleel,
the son of Cainan,
38 the son of Enos,
the son of Seth,
the son of Adam,
the son of God.'

Redaction

[23a] This verse comes from Luke; similarly, 'as was supposed' is an interjection of the redactor, who now wants to introduce a genealogy constructed on physical descent without dropping the virgin birth which he has previously reported (as is well known, we find similar redactional work in Matt. 1.16f.; cf. above, pp. 62f.).

Tradition

As is shown by the tracing back of the genealogy to God, it probably comes from circles which were concerned not only – like the author of the Matthaean genealogy – to demonstrate that Jesus was the son of David and Abraham but above all to depict Jesus as the goal and consummation of salvation history.

As Joseph is regarded as the father of Jesus without any qualification, at the time of the composition of the genealogy the virgin birth was evidently still outside the field of vision.

There are Old Testament parallels e.g. in Gen. 5.3–32 and 11.10–26.

History

The fact that they are largely incompatible (they agree to some extent only in the generations from Abraham to David, because both follow the Old Testament; cf. Ruth 4.18–22; I Chron. 2.1–14) tells against the historical reliability of the genealogies in Matthew and Luke:

(a) Matthew traces the genealogy from David through Solomon and Luke through Nathan;

(b) Shealtiel and his son Zerubbabel certainly appear in both genealogies (Matt. 1.12; Luke 3.27), but whereas Luke mentions nineteen names in all between Zerubbabel and Jesus, in Matthew there are only ten;

(c) The name of Jesus' grandfather is already uncertain (Matt. 1.15f.: Jacob; Luke 3.23: Eli).

The reference to the authenticity of other contemporary genealogies and the great civic and religious value that people generally attached to the preservation of traditions about the legitimacy of descent (Jeremias 1969: 297) cannot alter the verdict that neither the Matthaean nor the Lukan genealogy is based on historically reliable accounts. This would explain only the *interest* that led to the composition of the genealogy of Jesus.

Luke 4.16–30
Jesus' preaching in Nazareth

'16 And he came to *Nazareth, where he had been brought up*; and he went *as his custom was* to the synagogue on the sabbath day. *And he stood up to read. 17 And there was given to him the book of the prophet Isaiah. He opened the book and found the place where it was written:*

"18 The Spirit of the Lord is upon me,
because he has anointed me
to preach good news to the poor.
He has sent me
to proclaim release to the captives
and recovering of sight to the blind,
to set at liberty those who are oppressed,
19 to proclaim the acceptable year of the Lord."

20 *And he closed the book, and gave it back to the attendant, and sat down; and the eyes of all in the synagogue were fixed on him.*
21 *And he began to say to them, "Today this scripture has been fulfilled in your hearing."*
22 And *all spoke well of him, and* wondered at the *gracious words which proceeded* out of his mouth; and they said, "Is not this *Joseph's son?*"
23 *And he said to them, "Doubtless you will quote to me this proverb, 'Physician, heal yourself; what we have heard you did at Capernaum, do here in your ancestral city.'"* 24

And he said, "*Truly, I say to you*, no prophet is *welcome* in his ancestral city.

25 But in truth, I tell you, there were many widows in Israel in the days of Elijah, when the heaven was shut up three years and six months, when there came a great famine over all the land; 26 and Elijah was sent to none of them but only to Zarephath, in the land of Sidon to a woman who was a widow.

27 And there were many lepers in Israel in the time of the prophet Elisha; and none of them was cleansed, but only Naaman the Syrian."

28 *When they heard this, all in the synagogue were filled with wrath. 29 And they rose up and put him out of the city, and led him to the brow of the hill on which their city was built, that they might throw him down headlong. 30 But passing through the midst of them he went away.*'

Redaction

This section – which reworks Mark 6 – programmatically presents Jesus' inaugural preaching in his home town in Nazareth. Within the Gospel of Luke it stands where Mark narrates the call of the first disciples (Mark 1.16–20). Thus by deliberately dispensing with a chronological order, Luke puts a typical event at the head: the rejection of Jesus in Nazareth points forward to his later fate.

At the same time Luke extends the Markan passage at three points: *first* with a prophetic testimony put on the lips of Jesus in vv.18f.; *secondly* with the prophecy of the offer of salvation to the Gentiles in vv.25–27; and *thirdly* with a redactional conclusion to the event, which shows in anticipation the fate that Jesus is to expect.

[16] The basis of the verse is Mark 6.1f. Luke identifies Jesus 'ancestral city' with Nazareth because he had read in Mark 1.9 that Jesus had come from Nazareth in Galilee.

[17–20] The words that are read aloud by Jesus correspond to Isa.61.1–2.

[21] The link between history and scripture is redactionally important. Whereas in Mark the 'time' was fulfilled (Mark 1.15) and the rule of God was imminent (ibid.), in Luke there is a shift. *At that time* – in the time of Jesus – scripture was fulfilled. Similarly, the hostility of Jesus' fellow-citizens is a historicizing reference to his passion.

[22] In Luke, Mark's 'son of Mary' (6.3) becomes the son of Joseph. The mention of Jesus' brothers and sisters is omitted.

[23] This is to be explained as a deliberate composition by Luke. Consistently historicizing, Luke refers to Jesus' future actions in Capernaum which will be narrated next.

[24] Luke deletes not only the kinsfolk from the series of three in Mark 6.4, as does Matthew, but also the house; if in Mark the prophet is 'without honour', here he is 'not welcome'.

[25–27] These verses are nasty anti-Jewish polemic on the part of Luke. Salvation is leaving the Jews for the Gentiles (cf. similarly Matt. 8.11f.). At this point the opposition is already between Israel and the Gentiles (= Sidon, Syria). Two passages from the Old Testament are cited to indicate that the activity of a prophet benefits the members of an alien people instead of his own fellow-countrymen.

[28–30] These verses show how Luke wanted vv.25–27 to be understood. Jesus' Jewish compatriots are irredeemably lost, as is evident from their wrath against Jesus. Salvation *must* go to the Gentiles (cf. also the conclusion of Acts).

Tradition

[18–19] The words corresponding to Isa.61.1f. are put on the lips of Jesus in the framework of early Christian development of the Old Testament notion of fulfilment.

History

[18–19] Jesus did not speak Isa.61.1f. for the simple reason that the verses are quoted in the Septuagint version.

[25–27] These verses are unhistorical, as Jesus did not carry on any mission to the Gentiles.

As everything else has been developed on the basis of the Markan account, for the historical question see the Markan pericope and the analysis of it (above, pp. 54f.).

Luke 8.19–21
Jesus' true kinsfolk

> 19 Then his mother and his brothers came to him, but they could not reach him for the crowd. 20 And he was told, "Your mother and your brothers are standing outside, and want to see you." 21 But he said to them. "My mother and my brothers are those who *hear* the *word* of God *and* do it."'

Redaction

This section has been detached from the context in which it appears in Mark (cf. Mark 3.31–35). Luke's point corresponds to Mark's. The true kinsfolk of Jesus are those who hear and do God's word (Mark 3.5: those who do the will of God). Luke (like Matthew) deletes Mark 3.21 to tone the statement down.

Tradition and history

The yield is nil (cf. above, p. 48 on Mark 3.31–35).

Luke 11.27–28
A beatitude on the mother of Jesus

> '27 *As he said this, a woman in the crowd raised her voice and said to him,* "Blessed is the womb that bore you, and the breasts that you sucked!" 28 *But he said, "Blessed rather are those who hear the word of God and keep it!"'*

Redaction

The occasion for this beatitude in the context of the Gospel of Luke is the preceding exorcism of demons (v.14). Whereas this provokes a negative reaction among the crowd (vv.15f.), for the woman it indicates the greatness of Jesus. Jesus' answer is to be understood, on the basis of 1.48 (see above, pp. 104f.), more as a correction than as a strict repudiation of the beatitude. The question whether the mother of Jesus is to be called blessed is not ultimately decisive. What is important for the disciples is, rather, hearing and doing the word of God. To this degree the relationship between vv.27 and 28 corresponds to the first and second parts of the question in Luke 6.46: 'Why do you call me "Lord, Lord" and do not do what I say?').

Tradition and history

The yield is nil.

Acts 1.14
Mary in the primitive community

> 'All these (viz. the disciples) devoted themselves to prayer, together with the women and Mary, the mother of Jesus, and her brothers.'

Redaction

This verse expands on what has gone before, by saying that after the ascension of Jesus the eleven apostles were not alone, but were harmoniously gathered with their wives in the upper room. The whole passage is an idyll. Here Luke is depicting a kind of holy primitive community which consists of the families of the disciples and the family of the Lord, in a scheme with a chiastic construction: men (= twelve apostles) – their wives/women (= Mary the mother of Jesus)

– men (= the brothers of Jesus). Accordingly, Acts 1.14 is to be seen in parallel to the family stories in Luke 1–2. It also follows that Acts 1.14 goes back to Luke in its entirety.

Tradition and history

The yield is nil.

The Gospel of John

John 1.12–13
The origin of the children of God

> '12 But to all who received him, who believed in his name, he gave power to become children of God; 13 who were engendered, not of blood nor of the will of the flesh nor of the will of man, but of God.'

These two verses are part of the prologue to the Gospel of John, which narrates the pre-existence and the incarnation of the Logos. They depict the reception of Jesus as the word (Logos) by human beings and contain a striking threefold negation concerning the 'children of God': (they are) engendered neither from blood nor from the will of the flesh nor from the will of a man. This corresponds precisely to the faith of the church about the birth of Jesus, except that in this faith the birth from a virgin is explicitly reported. From this we are to conclude one of two things. Either John is alluding to the birth of Jesus and thinks that the birth of Christians, which takes place without blood and is rooted only in God, follows the birth of Christ himself. Or this statement in vv.12–13 is to be explained from the religious context, in which the presuppositions of birth from a virgin, fathering by God, were developed. Since the Gospel of John in all probability presupposes the Gospel of Luke (cf. Lüdemann 1994: 151–74), the former possibility is to be preferred.

John 1.45
Jesus, the son of Joseph

'Philip found Nathanael, and said to him, "We have found him of whom Moses in the law and also the prophets wrote, Jesus the son of Joseph, the one from Nazareth."'

The verse stands within the section John 1.35–51, which depicts the calling of the first disciples and presupposes Mark 1.16–20. John has considerably expanded the scene and has partly changed both the sequence and the names of the disciples. Whereas in Mark Jesus first called the brothers Simon and Andrew (1.16–18), and then James and John the sons of Zebedee (1.19f), in the Gospel of John Andrew and an unnamed disciple, Simon, Philip and finally Nathanael follow one another.

Tradition and history

The evangelist speaks of Jesus as son of Joseph (as in John 6.42, see below, p. 131). This corresponds to the general tendency of the early Christian tradition to move from the designation of Jesus as son of Mary to the designation 'son of Joseph'. John 8.41 shows what this tendency of the early Christian tradition is directed *against*. Like Mark 6.3, this text reflects the earliest stratum in the history of tradition: Jesus was fathered by someone other than his mother's later husband and is therefore named after her.

John 2.1–12
The miracle with the wine at the wedding in Cana

'1 *On the third day* there was a marriage at Cana in Galilee, and the mother of Jesus was there; 2 Jesus also was invited to the marriage, with his disciples. 3 When the wine ran out, the mother of Jesus said to him, "They have no (more) wine."'

4 And Jesus said to her, "Woman, what have you to do with me? My hour has not yet come."

5 His mother said to the servants, "Do what he tells you." 6 Now six stone jars were standing there, for the Jewish (rites of) purification, each holding two or three measures. 7 Jesus said to them, "Fill the jars with water." And they filled them up to the brim. 8 He said to them, "Now draw some out, and take it to the steward of the feast." So they took it.

9 When the steward of the feast tasted the water now become wine, and did not know where it came from (*though the servants who had drawn the water knew*), the steward of the feast called the bridegroom 10 and said to him, "Every man serves the good wine first; and when men have drunk freely, then the poor wine; but you have kept the good wine until now."

11 This, the first of his signs, Jesus did at Cana in Galilee, *and revealed his glory*; and his disciples believed in him.

12 After this he went down to Capernaum, with his mother and his brothers and his disicples, and there they stayed for a few days.'

Redaction

[1] The note 'on the third day' corresponds to 1.29, 35, 43 and derives from John's historicizing tendency. The mother of Jesus, whose name John does not give either here or later, appears here for the first time in the Gospel.

[2] The mention of the disciples refers back to the scenes of their calling in John 1.35–51.

[3] This verse creates the first presupposition for the miracle. Mary points out to Jesus that the wine has run out and thus implicitly expresses her wish for him to see to new wine.

[4] The form of address 'Woman' which Jesus uses to his mother (cf. similarly 19.26) does not lack respect, but it is not particularly respectful either. Later he uses this same distant form of address to a Samaritan woman (4.21) and to Mary

Magdalene (20.13,15). The form of address and the dismissive phrase 'What have you to do with me?' are made more understandable by the addition 'My hour has not yet come.' That means that Jesus' actions are not governed by human wishes and motives: he (or his heavenly Father) alone determines what he does. The fact that in vv.7–8 Jesus then seems to accede to his mother's implicit request is not a contradiction for John. In a similar way, in John 7.1–13 Jesus initially rejects his brothers' request for him to go to Jerusalem and reveal himself to the world ('My time is not yet come', John 7.8), but then secretly follows them. At the same time the word 'hour' mysteriously already points forward to the hour of Jesus' death and his glorification (John 7.30; 8.20; 12.23,27; 13.1; 17.1).

[5] The request to the servants to obey the words of Jesus shows that despite the negative reaction of her son, Mary will not be dissuaded from her certainty that he will help in some way.

[6] The mention of the stone jars creates the second presupposition for the miracle, which is then reported indirectly.

[7–8] Here there is no mention of the actual miraculous event.

[9–10] The tasting of the wine by the steward of the feast and the humorous proverb serve as public confirmation of the miracle.

[11] The numbering of this miracle as the first, that Jesus did in Cana, points forward to the healing of the son of the royal official which is designated the second (4.54). 'And he revealed his glory' is Johannine terminology.

[12] This verse bridges the time up to the Passover feast as the background of the following narrative.

Tradition and history

Form-critically, John 1.2–12 is based on a typical miracle story, the original form of which did not mention the mother of Jesus. Her inclusion in the narrative reflects the reputation she had in the Johannine communities.

Neither the framework of the action nor the miracle with the wine have a historical background.

John 6.42
Jesus, the son of Joseph

'Is not this Jesus, the son of Joseph, whose father and mother we know? How can he now say that he has come down from heaven?'

Redaction

The first of the two questions asked by the Jews is like the question of Jesus' fellow-countrymen in Mark 6.3. In Mark it is prompted by the wisdom and miracles of Jesus; in John by his own testimony that he has come down from heaven.

Although John nowhere explicitly attests belief in the virgin birth of Jesus, he probably knew it and accepted it (see above on 1.12–13). To this degree the verse serves to show the stubbornness of the Jews: as the truth about Jesus' origin is hidden from them, they do not understand that it is completely in accord with this testimony that he has come down from heaven.

Tradition and history

Cf. above pp. 50–60 on Mark 6.3 and p. 128 on John 1.45.

John 8.41
Jesus – born of fornication?

'"You do the works of your father." They said to him, "We were not born of fornication; we have one Father, God."'

Redaction

The join between v.41 and what has preceded it is harsh, since the topic of freedom developed in John 8.30–40, which is connected with being a child of Abraham, is not continued in vv.41–45.

The saying of Jesus with which the verse begins pre-supposes that the Jews, who as representatives of the world represent non-believers, call themselves children of God. Only v.44 explicitly says who Jesus means by their real father, namely the devil. However, here already the Jews rightly understand the allusion as an attack on their claim to be children of God. Therefore they emphasize that God alone is their father. Conversely, by rejecting a birth in fornication with an emphatic 'not us', they accuse Jesus of having been born in adultery. Thus they counter the questioning of their religious integrity with the criticism that Jesus is illegitimate.

Consequently, without knowing it, according to John at the same time they speak the truth about Jesus' birth. He was not in fact born of a human act. But what the hardened Jews depict as birth in fornication is reality his origin from God.

Tradition and history

The scene which according to John frames the dialogue between Jesus and the Jews is certainly fictitious; however, the insinuation of the Jews contains the tradition which is also reflected in Mark 6.3: Jesus' birth was illegitimate.

John 19.25–27
The mother of Jesus and the Beloved Disciple beneath the cross

'25 But standing by the cross of Jesus were his mother, and his mother's sister, Mary the wife of Clopas, and Mary Magdalene. 26 When Jesus saw his mother, and the disciple whom he loved standing near, he said to his mother, "Woman, behold your son." 27 Then he said to the disciple, "Behold, your mother!" And from that hour the disciple took her to his own home.'

Redaction

[25] In view of the precise enumeration of the women which surprisingly also include the mother of Jesus, it is striking that
[26f.] here the Beloved Disciple, who had not been mentioned at all previously, is by the cross.

This indicates a redactional seam: accordingly John may have added vv.26f. to v.25, which was in the tradition, and also expanded this with the figure of Mary.

Tradition

Verse 25 comes from tradition; vv.26f. are essentially an element of the tradition, which originally had nothing to do with the death of Jesus. It brings Mary and the Beloved Disciple together (cf. Günther 1996: 64). In that case the evangelist dramatized the scene by associating it with Jesus' last hours. (Cf. the pericope of the cleansing of the temple, John 2.13–25, which against all historical probability the evangelist has put chronologically in quite a different place from the Synoptics, at the beginning of Jesus' activity.)

History

In view of the reports in the Synoptic Gospels the scene cannot make any claim to historicity. The reasons for this are:
(a) In Mark 15.40f. par. the women observe the event *from afar*;
(b) the mother of Jesus does not appear in any of the lists in the Synoptic Gospels;
(c) John puts the women directly under the cross;

133

(d) he inserts Mary the mother of Jesus without naming her directly;

(e) the evangelist adds the scene with the Beloved Disciple and among the women is interested only in the mother of Jesus, who is not directly named.

Conclusion: for traditio-critical and source-critical reasons it cannot be assumed that Mary, the mother of Jesus, stood under the cross.

The Gospel of Thomas

Logion 105
Jesus – son of the harlot?

> 'Jesus said, "He who knows the father and the mother will be called 'son of the harlot'."'

In this logion Jesus is probably talking about himself and his special relationship to his father and his mother. The following passages from the Gospel of Thomas can serve as illustrations.

> 61.3: 'I am He who comes forth from the one who is the same; things of my father have been given to me.'
> 101.3 '[My] true [mother], she gave me life.'

Jesus' sayings about his father and his mother are meant both literally and metaphorically. How does this relate to the second part of logion 105?

Jesus, who knows his father and his mother, is called 'son of the harlot'. This statement evidently takes up the tradition which is also reflected in John 8.41 and which from the beginning was reported by non-Christian Jews against the birth of Jesus. Here 'harlot' may be exaggerated polemic against the illegitimate birth of Jesus.

Protevangelium of James

The so-called Protevangelium of James, which was of great significance in the development of the dogma of the perpetual virginity of Mary, has come down to us more or less intact in a large number of Greek manuscripts, the earliest of which, Bodmer Papyrus V (third/fourth century), was only published in 1958, and in numerous translations.

While it presupposes the canonical infancy narratives, it makes very free use of the stories known from the Gospels of Matthew and Luke, probably partly from oral tradition (e.g. it speaks of the birth of Jesus in a cave near Bethlehem). Mary comes from the upper class and is born not in a Jewish village but in Jerusalem (5,2). Perhaps here the author is answering a Jewish claim that Mary was of lowly descent (cf. Schaberg 1994: 720). Since the church father Origen certainly used the Protevangelium at the beginning of the third century and Justin around 150 CE agrees with some of its teachings (birth in the cave, *Dial.* 78,5; Davidic descent of Mary, *Dial.* 43,1; 45,4; 100,3, etc.), it can be dated to before the end of the second century. The alleged author is James, who would have written the book after the death of Herod the Great (4 BCE) or Herod Agrippa (44 CE).

The Protevangelium above all reports the miraculous birth of *Mary*. However, the continuing virginity of Mary even during and after the birth of *Jesus* is vividly confirmed by the following story:

Protevangelium of James 19.3–20.3
The proof of the Mary's virginity

'19.3 And the midwife came out of the cave (viz. in which Jesus was born), and Salome met her. And she said to her: "Salome, Salome, I have a new sight to tell you; a virgin has brought forth, a thing which her nature does not allow."

And Salome said: "As (truly Lord my God lives, unless

I put forward) my finger and test her condition, I will not believe that a virgin has brought forth."

20.1 And the midwife went in and said to Mary: "Make yourself ready, for there is no small contention concerning you." And when Mary heard this, she made herself ready. And Salome put forward her finger to test her condition. And she cried out, saying: "Woe for my wickedness and my unbelief; for I have tempted the living God; and behold, my hand falls away from me, consumed by fire!"

2 And Salome bowed her knees before the Lord, saying: "O God of my fathers, remember me; for I am the seed of Abraham, Isaac and Jacob; do not make me a public example to the children of Israel, but restore me to the poor. For you know, Lord, that in your name I perform my duties and from you I have received my hire."

3. And behold, an angel of the Lord stood [before Salome] and said to her: "Salome, God the Lord has heard your prayer. Stretch out your hand to the child and touch him (take him in your arms), so will healing and joy be yours."

4 And full of joy Salome came to the child, touched him, [and said: "I will worship him, for (in him) a great king has been born to Israel"]. And Salome was healed at once [as she had requested], and she went out of the cave [justified]. And behold, an angel of the Lord [a voice] cried: "Salome, Salome, tell [not] what marvel you have seen, before the child comes to Jerusalem"' (text following Schneemelcher 1991: 434f., textual variants in square brackets).

The Protevangelium of James reflects the popular piety which first gave rise to the formation of the dogma of the perpetual virginity of Mary. It as it were highlights the way in which virginity was understood: it was measured by the presence of the hymen, which remained intact at the birth of Jesus.

The doctrine of the perpetual virginity of Mary might be the most important dogma about the figure of Mary, even more important than the divine motherhood. The virginity of

Mary is the basis of all later speculations about the special privileges and graces which were ascribed to her. Even the Roman Catholic interpretation of the divine motherhood depends on the perpetual virginity; but this is especially the case with the dogmas of the immaculate conception and the physical assumption, which would be impossible without the perpetual virginity, since they both presuppose that Mary's body remained undamaged by sin and incorruptible.

The history of the tradition. How it developed

The earliest statement about the mother of Jesus in the tradition does not mention her. Jesus was born of a woman – thus Paul's statement, which could imagine the birth of the son of God only 'chastely', i.e. from a married woman. At the same time, as mother of Jesus Mary gained a certain place of honour in the early church – thus in the Gospel of John, in which for this reason she no longer needed to be mentioned by name.

The next stage (Mark) reflects a problem in the origin of Jesus and historically takes us behind Paul. Jesus is described as son of a mother who is now mentioned by name. This compellingly presupposes criticism of a dishonourable origin and puts the finger on a sore point: the lack of mention of a father, which automatically put the mother in the shade (thus also the tradition presupposed in John 8.41 and Gospel of Thomas 105). Mark already neutralizes this by adding a family catalogue, and all the Gospels which follow him (Matthew, Luke, John) immediately delete the expression 'son of Mary'. Now Jesus is officially son of Joseph; the historical basis of this may be that Joseph in fact adopted Mary's son. The genealogies in the Gospels, the tradition about Jesus as son of David presupposed by Paul in Rom.1.3f., and the Christmas stories in the Gospels are based on this. But both display a clearly recognizable rift: Luke 1.26–38 introduces Joseph as father into the narrative at what is clearly a later stage, whereas Luke 2.1–20 presupposes Joseph's paternity without question. While Matthew sings the praise of Joseph in his Christmas story, at the same time the Gospel feels occasioned to do away with the ugly rumour of Jesus' illegitimacy.

The scornful comment in Mark about 'son of Mary' is rooted in Jewish criticism of Jesus' origin which was already directed against him (and his followers) during his lifetime and was intensified after his 'resurrection'. It has a historical foundation in the fact that Jesus really did have another father than Joseph and was in fact fathered before Mary's marriage, presumably through rape.

Christology develops in parallel to this Jewish anti-criticism. Thus we already observe in Paul and Mark that Jesus is called son of God: in the tradition handed down by Paul in connection with his birth, in Mark first at his baptism. Then similar christological developments lead to the development of the theologoumenon of the virgin birth which Matthew and Luke already had before them and which had possibly been encouraged by the charge of illegitimate birth. This theologumenon of the virgin birth is found at a secondary level in the Greek translation of the Old Testament (Isa.7.14), as is so much else, although the Hebrew original does not speak of a virgin but of a young woman. Finally, the Protevangelium of James vividly endorses the virginity of Mary even after the birth of Jesus.

Diagram

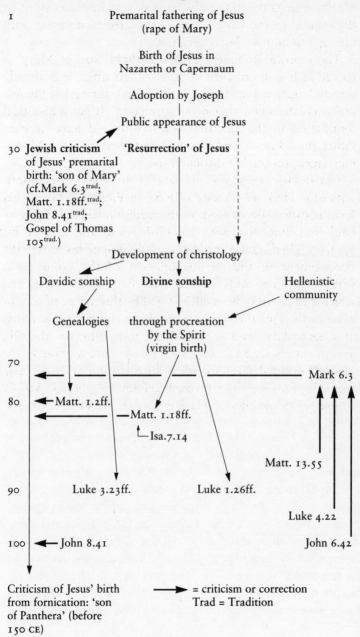

1   Premarital fathering of Jesus
    (rape of Mary)
    |
    Birth of Jesus in
    Nazareth or Capernaum
    |
    Adoption by Joseph
    |
    Public appearance of Jesus

30 **Jewish criticism**   'Resurrection' of Jesus
    of Jesus' premarital
    birth: 'son of Mary'
    (cf.Mark 6.3^trad;
    Matt. 1.18ff.^trad;
    John 8.41^trad;
    Gospel of Thomas
    105^trad.)

                Development of christology

    Davidic sonship   **Divine sonship**   Hellenistic
                                                  community

        Genealogies   through procreation
                       by the Spirit
                       (virgin birth)

70 ← — — — — — — — — — — — —   Mark 6.3

80 ← Matt. 1.2ff.

        ← — Matt. 1.18ff.
            └─ Isa.7.14

                                        Matt. 13.55

90   Luke 3.23ff.   Luke 1.26ff.

                                        Luke 4.22

100 ← John 8.41   John 6.42

Criticism of Jesus' birth   ——→ = criticism or correction
from fornication: 'son   Trad = Tradition
of Panthera' (before
150 CE)

139

3

Theological Results

The procedure

In this chapter I shall attempt to present some constructive theological conclusions on Mary and her son Jesus on the basis of the historical facts, while constantly taking account of the way in which they have been interpreted in the first two millennia. It is impossible here to offer a comprehensive survey of present-day mariology. I shall merely highlight some points which have become evident to me in reading the almost endless theological literature on Mary.

A clarification

First, however a firm line must be drawn. The statement that Jesus was engendered by the Spirit and born of a virgin is a falsification of the historical facts. At all events he had a human father. From that it follows, *first*, that any interpretation which fails to take a clear stand here is to be branded a lie. This includes all the official Catholic dogma about Mary, and also the confessions of Jesus as the virgin's son which are made every Sunday in Protestant worship. *Secondly*, comments by Protestant professors of theology who, together with their Catholic colleagues, fail to make any clear statement about the historicity of the virgin birth in any of their publications and prefer obscure formulations are also to be put under this heading. The fact that in the sphere of history all verdicts can only be probable is insufficient reason for being tolerant in questions of historical truth.

It goes without saying that at this point we also have to ask how we are to judge North American stars of biblical exegesis like R.E. Brown (1977, 1978), J.A. Fitzmyer (1981) and J.P. Meier (1991), who have occupied themselves with the birth of Jesus from a virgin more thoroughly than most others and in the end have not felt able to contradict Catholic dogma. Either they were too cowardly to do so, or they have allowed it to become second nature to live a spiritual ghetto existence, according to the principle 'when in doubt judge in favour of the church and its dogma' (for a brilliant criticism of Brown and Meier see Schaberg 1997: 55–61). Has it not become clear here that these scholars – like many of their Catholic colleagues in Germany – are simply apologists, whom one cannot trust to point the way?

The two roots of the virgin birth

The masquerade of the birth of Jesus from a virgin had two roots:

(a) It offered an answer to the version, meant as slander, that Jesus had been born out of wedlock as an illegitimate child and had been conceived in fornication.

(b) It put Jesus on a level with other divine heroes of antiquity, whose birth, because of their lofty status, can be attributed only to procreation by God or by an intermediary being.

Both 'answers' presuppose a high christology. To this degree statements about Mary are closely interlocked with the dogmatics of Jesus the risen Son of God. In other words, Mary as a saint is simply the other side of the coin of Jesus the Son of God. This notion of a father God and his son already carried with it the idea of a mother of God.

Mary – condemned to silence

But the ruins of history speak another language: the quite unholy, premarital and probably violent fathering of Jesus

141

immediately attracted the charge by his later adoptive father Joseph that Mary had conceived Jesus in fornication, whereas the desperate situation of the young woman Mary led to her complete silence. She does not, indeed may not, say anything about her pregnancy. Rather, from now on her womb – in reaction to the hostile pornographic insinuation – is made the place of a procreation without sexuality. Here gynaecology provides theology with the legitimation of the divine origin and lordship of Jesus.

The arsenal of christology

I remarked that mariology is grounded in christology. Now Protestants rightly complain that today in particular mariology has gone beyond all bounds. People seem to think that christology is required by the Bible, whereas mariology is not, or only to a modest degree. But that does not go far enough, if historical criticism is to have any consequences at all. Those who rightly complain about the flood of mariology should at the same time disarm themselves of their own christological arsenal. For what relationship is there between the man from Nazareth and the ruler of the world, as the later communities first made him, and as he is confessed in the church even today? Despite the changing historical situations over the centuries, Christianity's old claim to a share in his rule of the world can still be encountered today. This happens, as I have already said, in the simple recitation of creeds which confess the lordship of Christ over death and life. If this claim on the part of Christianity could still serve to legitimate secular rule in the Roman empire and throughout the Middle Ages, provided that such rule showed itself friendly towards the church, today it faces a serious problem: the democratic rather than religious legitimation of rule, the functional differentiation within our modern societies and the end of the Christian monopoly in the religious market.

Granted, today the churches are pleading for a love of neighbour which is practised symbolically, but not necessarily in a political way. However, without expressly saying so, they cling on to the idea of participation in the rule of Christ. At all events, here missionary action is thus practised as social action. That is certainly better than a mission with fire and sword. But it makes ethical action an instrument of the higher Christian aim of establishing the rule of Christ.

Liberation theology and the rule of Christ

Liberation theologians and also the World Council of Churches have spoken more clearly about this combination of ethics and rule. In countries of the so-called Third World love of neighbour appears in the garb of liberation theology. There whole churches take the side of the oppressed and get caught up in the militant terror and persecutions of the exploited countries. The bold practice of liberation theologians creates a protected space and option for action on behalf of the poorest of the poor, taking sides in their emergency. Nevertheless, at its roots this theology has not revised its theological claim to power. Despite the great commitment of these theologians, we must be allowed to ask whether at the structural theological level, once again an unbroken old claim to rule is not being presented in new garb. Is religious legitimation once again simply being given to political power, this time that of the oppressed? Unfortunately Karl Barth's talk of the revelation of God in Jesus Christ as the Lord has also hindered rather than helped a critical grappling with Christians' own claim to rule.

The functionalization of Mary as an example of liberation theology

On the basis of cultural reflections Virgil Elizondo develops a mariology of liberation, with the figure of Mary as the model of an evangelizing ecumenism (1988: 131–41). Attention needs to be paid, not to the Mary of the Western cultural tradition but to Mary as mother and bearer of a new religious

143

and cultural symbiosis. The Mary who addressed the Indios in appearances is the basis for Latin American liberation theology.

In 1531, ten years after the subjection and missionizing of the native population of Mexico by white Christian Europeans, Mary appeared to Juan Diego, a despised Indio, who was on the way to church to be instructed about the things of God. Whereas previously the Spanish conquerors were regarded as the chosen servants and messengers of the true God, from then on Juan Diego became a missionary for the Spanish (135). The event of Guadalupe contributed to the liberation of the oppressed. Mary became the figure with whom Mexican people, who had been alienated from their roots by the Christian mission, could identify, and time and again she was important in the battle against despots. Thus in the 1920s the Cristeros in Mexico dedicated themselves to the Virgin of Guadalupe and in the long term succeeded in abolishing the dictatorship. In December 1931 more than half a million believers celebrated the 400th anniversary of the Virgin of Guadalupe with a gigantic festival.

Alongside political liberation Mary also brings liberation from sexual violence.

The virginity of Mary stands 'in opposition to the scandal and the shame of women who have been raped. Mary was pure and unblemished because she had not been touched by the greedy hands of the conqueror. In her the Mexican woman has been given back her original dignity . . . What had been prostituted and shamed by the conqueror has now been virginized by God. In this case the virginity is a complete rehabilitation of dishonoured personal dignity' (137).

In liberation theology, the character of Marian piety as projection is seen as extraordinarily creative human energy. It shows itself in Mary as in a high flight against dark clouds.

The author compares this process with the conditions in

which Christianity came into being: Hellenized Christianity, which ushered in the evangelization of the whole of the Roman empire, opened up new horizons to Christianity through its universality (139).

Criticism: In so far as this interpretation is based on the psalm in the Lukan infancy narrative ('He casts down the mighty from their thrones' [Luke 1.52]), it is a forced interpretation, since Mary never spoke this verse. In so far as it acknowledges the character of the appearances of Mary as projections which rehabilitate personal dignity, there are no objections to it, even if in this way God as traditionally interpreted vanishes from the horizon and exclusively human forces are involved. For possibly 'God' is to be discovered in us in a completely new way. But here, too, the question arises of the relationship to history and to the text. And Hellenistic Christianity in particular, which emphasized the aspect of the subjection of powers by Christ (cf. Phil.2.5–11), then as now suffered from a lack of clarification of its own relationship to power and is hard to rediscover again in the message of Jesus.

Conclusion: This liberation theology has no support in the biblical texts about Mary and her son Jesus, however positively it may be rated as a creative development in connection with an appearance of Mary. It also remains to be noted that there were apparently no problems in using Mary in the great variety of theological contexts in Latin America past and present. The conquerors used her, and now the liberation theologians do the same. Who was Mary really? That is the question which such approaches should raise if they are not to stand naked before history and the biblical text.

Mary in feminist theology

In feminist theology (cf. the bibliography under Daly, Mulack, Schottroff and Schüssler Fiorenza), which can only be touched on here, and which I would want to protect from dogmatic criticism (cf. Grass 1991: 103–6; Maron 1988:

174–6), the observer is faced with three new entrances into the ancient theological building.

In front of the *first* door are women whose aim it is to use feminist theology to contribute towards a renewal of the structure of theology and the church, which needs cleaning. They aim at a community in the church which tolerates all the differences between women and men. It is their aim to live out a new quality of relationships in which women and men have equal rights and find God anew. They read the biblical texts with this intention to reform. They have been amazingly successful in working out the influence that Christian women already had at the beginning of Christianity. They also give a great deal of room within the church to the feminist interest in Christianity in the present and can enter the church door with a good conscience, to take up a lasting residence there. The price they pay for this is that they deal selectively with the biblical statements about Mary: they emphasize her humility and her special status given by God, but dispense with an examination of the facticity of the divine action in Mary's body. Incarnation and virginity continue to be the basis for Mary's lowliness and exaltation. Thus in the last resort they base themselves on and thereby support the traditional doctrines of the church.

In front of the *second* door stand women who see Christianity as deeply permeated by male fantasies. They not only note the misogynism of the texts but also take it seriously. They see no chance of finding a place in the Christian tradition by alternative readings. These women do not think that Christianity can be reformed, since its central statements of faith are patriarchal. Only rarely do they engage in historical research into the facts and instead prefer to make their own history. Thus Mary Daly founded a religion of her own in order to practise a post-Christian way of dealing with new sisterly forms of spirituality. The exodus from the patriarchal building takes place under the slogan: the way to freedom goes through the door and out of it again.

Behind the *third* door are gathered women who want to go

yet another way. Taking up biblical and church traditions, they discover completely new approaches to texts about Mary and interpret these against their allegedly matriarchal background or in terms of a matriarchal future. They elevate Mary and thus make her a key figure in the process of self-discovery among women with a Christian orientation in the present. This hermeneutical door may also appear to be an emergency exit from the rotten building of theology and the church – the unhistorical way of dealing with the biblical texts makes it a back door.

Thus, to sum up: the feminist concern to reform the structure of theology breaks off from the historical reconstruction of the life of Mary at the point at which the dogmatic pillars on which the structure rests would have to be broken up. Neither the radical feminist breaks with the Christian past nor their hermeneutical reinterpretations under the aegis of the goddess take the texts literally. Thus both groups *a priori* dispense with the critical potential of history and do not really hold up a mirror to tradition. But theologically, too, neither the humiliated nor the exalted Mary is viable, because both are indissolubly bound up with Jesus the ruler of the world. Mary precedes him as virgin, accompanies him as mother, sings his song of domination and ends as his bride. Here exaggerated expectations are projected on to the good woman in heaven and replace the power of all the old heavenly goddesses (cf. generally Benko 1993). In Mary they embody a programme which despises women and finally forces every woman into the role of saint or whore. Here son, male, ruler, wage-earner continue to be in the main roles.

The anthropological level of the appearances of Mary

A positive aspect of the abundance of appearances of Mary and speculations about Mary relates to the anthropological level. So its truth lies in the human sphere. If we begin from the assumption that our images of God are based on projections, the Christian God is constantly in danger of becoming a purely masculine being. But with the advent of the mother of God the Christian God became quasi-bisexual, and men and women could find themselves completely in him if they were allowed to project not only their male parts but also their female parts on to God.

Mary is therefore an image of the femininity of the divine and thus the human, just as the Logos Jesus is the image for the masculinity of God and thus the human. The depths of both dimensions have been and are perceived by human beings through appearances of Christ or Mary which are to be described as visions. The two poles are constants of human existence which have become evident to us in our lives. Human beings can only gain if both parts are affirmed equally completely and are as it were automatically integrated.

The historically unyielding aspect of Mary and her son Jesus

However, a general anthropological approach is only one aspect of interpretation. It is equally necessary to give history its due. In concrete, that means here that we must expose ourselves completely to the historical reality of that time and constantly keep in view the historical picture of Mary which has been stifled in the patriarchal system and not allowed to speak. Jesus, her son, embodies in his preaching and his activity something like the principle of protest, of criticism, and thus a potential which shatters any rigid systems based on domination. In him or in his immediate surroundings patriarchalism no longer plays a role: all are equal participants in the kingdom of God.

But even this spring of the appearance of Jesus did not last long. On the cross he experienced what loneliness, pain and godforsakenness means. His mother Mary endured similar experiences at the time when she conceived her child, the time of her pregnancy and the moment of giving birth to her son. From the beginning, the tradition of the Bible and the church could not bear this, and it immediately painted the story of Mary and her son Jesus against a golden background. Moreover theological dogmatics left the basis of history and built one castle in the air after another. In the course of church history, from the beginning until now, people destroyed everything which at that time was a bitter fact in order to be able to worship Jesus and Mary. But today we have no other possibility than to help to restore historical reality to life, because in the meantime almost everyone has come to know that the course of history was very different from that which the reports of the Bible and the church have related for centuries.

The tomb was full and the manger empty

Jesus' wretched tomb was full and his glorious manger was empty – that may be said to be the overall conclusion of my work. Despite the beautiful colours of the Bible, after such a prehistory holy night could only have been unholy for Mary. The silent night was cruel, noisy and hard. So it could not relieve the pain which had been inflicted on the young woman by a pregnancy which had been imposed on her in the truest sense of the word. The manger of a son of God born of a virgin, where homage was offered, had no place here, even if verses from the Bible, pious hymns and empty dogmatic formulae say it differently a thousand times. However, no one could guess who would really be born of Mary. For in Jesus there grew up the dream of someone who symbolically was to outdo all power in heaven and earth. He came to grief on the cross. His tomb remained full and was not replaced by the glory of the resurrection. Nevertheless, indeed precisely because of that, he has all my sympathy.

Bibliography

To save space, from the beginning works used are quoted in an abbreviated form, with the author's name and the date of publication of the edition used.

Archer, Léonie, *Her Price is Beyond Rubies. The Jewish Woman in Graeco-Roman Palestine*, JSOT.SS 60, 1990

Bach, Alice, *Women, Seduction and Betrayal in Biblical Narrative*, 1997

Barrett, Charles K., *The Gospel according to St John*, ²1978

Barth, Karl, *Die christliche Dogmatik im Entwurf. Erster Band. Die Lehre vom Worte Gottes*, 1927

Barth, Karl, *Church Dogmatics I/2, The Doctrine of the Word of God. Prolegomena to the Church Dogmatics*, ²1956

Barth, Karl, *Dogmatics in Outline* (1947), 1949

Bauer, Walter, *Das Leben Jesu im Zeitalter der neutestamentlichen Apokryphen* (1909), 1967

Bekenntnisschriften der evangelisch-lutherischen Kirche, ¹¹1992

Benko, Stephen, *The Virgin Goddess. Studies in the Pagan and Christian Roots of Mariology*, SHR LIX, 1993

Besier, Gerhard, *Konzern Kirche. Das Evangelium und die Macht des Geldes*, 1997

Billerbeck, Paul, *Kommentar zum Neuen Testament aus Talmud und Midrasch*, I–IV, 1969

Blinzler, Josef, *Die Brüder und Schwestern Jesu*, SBS 21, 1967

Børresen, Kari Elizabeth, 'Maria in der katholischen Theologie', in Moltmann-Wendel et al. 1988, 72–87

Bovon, François, *Das Evangelium nach Lukas (Lk 1,1–9,50)*, EKK III/1, 1989

Braun, Herbert, 'Der Sinn der neutestamentlichen Christologie' (1957), in id., *Gesammelte Studien zum Neuen Testament und seiner Umwelt*, 1971, 243–82

Brown, Raymond E., *The Birth of the Messiah. A Commentary on the Infancy Narratives in Matthew and Luke*, 1977, ²1993

Brown, Raymond E., Donfried, Karl P.,Fitzmyer, Joseph A. and Reumann, John, *Mary in the New Testament*, 1978

Bultmann, Rudolf, *The Gospel according to John*, 1971

Bultmann, Rudolf, *The History of the Synoptic Tradition*, Oxford ²1968

Campenhausen, Hans von, 'Die Jungfrauengeburt in der Theologie der alten Kirche' (1962), in id., *Urchristliches und Altkirchliches. Vorträge und Aufsätze*, 1979, 63–161

Catechism of the Catholic Church, 1994

Chadwick, Henry, *Origen: Contra Celsum. Translated with an Introduction and Notes*, ²1965

Chadwick, Henry and Evans, G.R., *Atlas of the Christian Church*, 1990

Conzelmann, Hans, *The Theology of St Luke*, London 1960

Crossan, John D., *The Historical Jesus. The Life of a Mediterranean Peasant*, 1993

Daly, Mary, *Beyond God the Father: Toward a Philosophy of Women's Liberation*, 1973

Dauer, Anton, *Die Passionsgeschichte im Johannesevangelium*, StANT 30, 1972

Delius, Walter, *Geschichte der Marienverehrung*, 1963

Denzinger, Heinrich and Schönmetzer, Adolf, *Enchiridion symbolorum, definitionum et declarationum de rebus fidei et morum*, ⁵⁶1976

Dibelius, Martin, 'Jungfrauensohn und Krippenkind. Untersuchungen zur Geburtsgeschichte Jesu im Lukas-Evangelium' (1932), in id., *Botschaft und Geschichte. Gesammelte Aufsätze* 1, ed. Günther Bornkamm, 1953, 1–78

Dibelius, Martin, *From Tradition to Gospel*, London 1934

Dinzelbacher, Peter (ed.), *Mittelalterliche Visionsliteratur. Eine Anthologie*, 1989

Elizondo, Virgil, 'Maria und die Armen. Ein Modell eines evangelisierenden Ökumenismus', in Moltmann-Wendel et al. 1988, 131–41

Emmerich, Anna Katharina, *Das Leben der heiligen Jungfrau Maria. Nach den Visionen der Augustinerin von Dülmen. Aufgeschrieben von Clemens Brentano*, ed. Arnold Guillet, ⁹1992

Fitzmyer, Joseph A., 'The Virginal Conception of Jesus in the New Testament', in id., *To Advance the Gospel. New Testament Studies*, 1981, 41–78

Gaventa, Beverly R., *Mary: Glimpses of the Mother of Jesus*, 1995

Gnilka, Joachim, *Das Matthäusevangelium, I. Teil (Kap. 1, 1–13, 58)*, HThK 1/1,1986

——, *Das Evangelium nach Markus, 1. Teilband. Mk 1–8, 26*, EKK lI/I, ³1989

Grass, Hans, *Traktat über Mariologie*, MThSt 30, 1991

Günther, Matthias, 'Der Ursprung der ephesinischen Marientradition. Zur Exegese von Joh 19,26f', in *Historische Wahrheit und theologische Wissenschaft. Gerd Lüdemann zum 50. Geburtstag*, ed. Alf Özen, 1996, 61–70

Härle, Wilfried, *Dogmatik*, 1995

Halkes, Catharina J.M., 'Maria – inspirierendes oder abschreckendes Vorbild für Frauen?', in Moltmann-Wendel et al. 1988, 113–30

Hanauer, Josef, ' "Muttergottes-Erscheinungen". Tatsachen oder Täuschungen?*, 1996

——, *Wunder oder Wundersucht? Erscheinungen, Visionen, Prophezeiungen, Besessenheit*, 1997

Harnack, Adolf, 'Das apostolische Glaubensbekenntnis, ein geschichtlicher Bericht nebst einer Einleitung und einemNachwort' (1892), in id., *Reden und Aufsätze* I, 1904, 219–64

Hase, Karl von, *Handbuch der Protestantischen Polemik gegen die Römisch-Katholische Kirche*, ⁶1894

Hirsch, Emanuel, *Das Wesen des Christentums*, 1939

——, *Frühgeschichte des Evangeliums. Zweites Buch. Die Vorlagen des Lukas und das Sondergut des Matthäus*, 1941

Hirsch, Emanuel, *Christliche Rechenschaft*, Erster Band, 1989

Ilan, Tal, ' "Man born of woman . . ." (Job 14:1). The Phenomenon of Men Bearing Metronymes at the Time of Jesus', *NT* XXXIV, 23–45

Jeremias, Joachim, *Jerusalem in the Time of Jesus. An Investigation into Economic and Social Conditions during the New Testament Period*, 1969

——, *Die Sprache des Lukasevangeliums. Redaktion und Tradition im Nicht-Markusstoff des dritten Evangeliums*, KEK Sonderband, 1980

Joest, Wilfried, *Dogmatik 1, Die Wirklichkeit Gottes*, 1989

Johnson, Marshall D., *The Purpose of the Biblical Genealogies with Special Reference to the Setting of the Genealogies of Jesus*, MSSNTS, ²1988

Keller, Werner, *The Bible as History*, 1956

Kiessig, Manfred (ed.), *Maria, die Mutter unseres Herrn. Eine evangelische Handreichung*, 1991

Klostermann, Erich, *Das Lukasevangelium*, HNT 5, ²1929

Krauss, Samuel, *Das Leben Jesu nach jüdischen Quellen*, 1902

Krötke, Wolf, 'Die Christologie Karl Barths als Beispiel für den Vollzug seiner Exegese', in Trowitzsch, Michael (ed.), *Karl Barths Schriftauslegung*, 1996, 1–21

Küng, Hans, *Credo. The Apostles' Creed Explained for Today*, 1993

Laurentin, René, *Lourdes: Histoire authentique des apparitions. I: Structure des témoignages. État de la question*, 1961 (six volumes appeared between 1961–1964)

Lüdemann, Gerd, *Early Christianity according to the Traditions in Acts. A Commentary*, 1989

——, *The Resurrection of Jesus. History, Experience, Theology*, 1995

——, *Heretics. The Other Side of Early Christianity*, 1996

——, *The Unholy in Holy Scripture. The Dark Side of the Bible*, 1997

Luther, Martin, *Kritische Gesamtausgabe* (= WA), Weimar 1883ff.

Luz, Ulrich, *Das Evangelium nach Matthäus (Mt 1–7)*, EKK Ill, 1992

Maier, Johann, *Jesus von Nazareth in der talmudischen Überlieferung*, 1978

Maron, Gottfried, *Zum Gespräch mit Rom. Beiträge aus evangelischer Sicht*, BensH 69, 1988

McArthur, Harvey K, '"Son of Mary"', *NT* XV, 1973, 38–58

McHugh, John, *The Mother of Jesus in the New Testament*, 1975

Meier, John P., *A Marginal Jew. Rethinking the Historical Jesus, Volume I, The Roots of the Problem and the Person*, 1991

Moltmann, Jürgen, 'Gibt es eine ökumenische Mariologie?', in Moltmann-Wendel et al., 1988, 14–22

——, *The Way of Jesus Christ. Christology in Messianic Dimensions*, 1990

Moltmann-Wendel, Elisabeth, Küng, Hans, and Moltmann, Jürgen (eds.), *Was geht uns Maria an? Beiträge zur Auseinandersetzung in Theologie, Kirche und Frömmigkeit*, GTB 493, 1988

Mulack, Christa, *Maria. Die geheime Göttin im Christentum*, ²1986

Neumann, Erich, *Zur Psychologie des Weiblichen*, Geist und Psyche, 1983

Neusner, Jacob, *The Mother of the Messiah in Judaism. The Book of Ruth*, 1993

Nigg, Walter, *Geschichte des religiösen Liberalismus*, 1937

Noland, John, 'The Four (Five) Women and Other Annotations in Matthew's Genealogy', *NTS* 43, 1997, 527–39

Norden, Eduard, *Die Geburt des Kindes. Geschichte einer religiösen Idee*, 1924 (= 1969)

Noth, Martin, *Numbers*, OTL, 1968

Pannenberg, Wolfhart, *The Apostles' Creed in the Light of Today's Questions*, 1972

Pelikan, Jaroslav, *Mary Through the Centuries*, 1996

Petersen, F., *Die wunderbare Geburt des Heilandes*, RGV 1/17,1909

Philo, *Complete Works*, Loeb Classical Library, 1929–43

Räisänen, Heikki, *Die Mutter Jesu im Neuen Testament*, AASF B 247, ²1989

Rahner, Karl, *Visions and Prophecies*, QD 10, 1963

——, '*Virginitas in partu*. A Contribution to the Development of Dogma and Tradition', in id., *Theological Investigations* 4, 1966, 134–62

Reik, Theodor, 'Dogma und Zwangsidee. Eine psycho-analytische Studie zur Entwicklung der Religion', *Imago* 13, 1927, 247–382

Rosa, Peter de, *Der Jesus-Mythos. Über die Krise des christlichen Glaubens*, 1991

Schaberg, Jane, *The Illegitimacy of Jesus. A Feminist Theological Interpretation of the Infancy Narratives*, 1987

——, 'The Infancy of Mary of Nazareth', in Elisabeth Schüssler Fiorenza (ed.), *Searching the Scriptures, Volume II: A Feminist Commentary*, 1994, 708–27

——, 'Feminist Interpretations of the Infancy Narrative of Matthew', *Journal of Feminist Studies in Religion* 13, 1997, 35–62

——, 'A Feminist Experience of Historical-Jesus Scholarship', in William E. Arnal and Michel Desjardins (eds), *Whose Historical Jesus?*, 1997, 146–60

Schlichting, Günter, *Ein jüdisches Leben Jesu*, WUNT 24, 1982

Schlink, Edmund, *Ökumenische Dogmatik. Grundzüge*, 1983

Schneemelcher, Wilhelm and Wilson, Robin McL. (eds.), *New Testament Apocrypha, Vol.1, Gospels*, ²1991

Schneider, Gerhard, *Das Evangelium nach Lukas. Kapitel 1–10*, ÖTK 3/1, 1977

Schottroff, Luise and Stegemann, Wolfgang, *Jesus von Nazareth – Hoffnung der Armen*, 1978

Schottroff, Luise, *Befreiungserfahrungen. Studien zur Sozialgeschichte des Neuen Testaments*, ThB 82, 1990

——, *Lydia's Impatient Sisters. A Feminist Social History of Early Christianity*, 1996

Schürer, Emil, *Geschichte des jüdischen Volkes im Zeitalter Jesu Christi*, I, 1901; II,1907; III,1909 (reissued 1964)

——, *The History of the Jewish People in the Age of Jesus Christ (175 BC–AD 135), A New English Version Revised and Edited by G. Vermes and F. Millar*, Vol.1,1973; Vol.2, 1979; Vol.3.1; Vol.3.2, 1987

Schüssler-Fiorenza, Elisabeth, *Jesus. Miriam's Child, Sophia's Prophet. Critical Issues in Feminist Christology*, 1995

Seeberg, Reinhold, 'Die Herkunft der Mutter Jesu', in *Theo-*

logische Festschrift für G. Nathanael Bonwetsch zu seinem 70. Geburtstage (17.Februar 1918), 1918, 13–24

Smend, Rudolf, 'Hat die Bibel wirklich recht?', in id., *Bibel, Theologie, Universität. Sechzehn Beiträge,* 1997, 41–5

Smith, Morton, *Jesus the Magician,* 1978

Spong, John Shelby, *Born of a Woman. A Bishop Rethinks the Birth of Jesus,* 1992

Stauffer, Ethelbert, 'Jeschu ben Mirjam. Kontroversgeschichtliche Anmerkungen zu Mk 6:3', in *Neotestamentica et Semitica. Studies in Honour of Matthew Black,* ed. E. Earle Ellis and Max Wilcox, 1969, 119–28

Stegemann, Hartmut, '"Die des Uria". Zur Bedeutung der Frauennamen in der Genealogie Matthäus 1, 1–17', in *Tradition und Glaube. Das frühe Christentum in seiner Umwelt. Festgabe für Karl Georg Kuhn zum 65. Geburtstag,* ed. Gert Jeremias, Heinz-Wolfgang Kuhn and Hartmut Stegemann, 1971, 246–76

Strack, Hermann L., *Jesus, die Häretiker und die Christen nach den ältesten jüdischen Angaben,* 1910

Strauss, David Friedrich, *The Life of Jesus* (1836), 1972

——, *Die christliche Glaubenslehre in ihrer geschichtlichen Entwicklung und im Kampfe mit der modernen Wissenschaft,* Vol.1, 1840; Vol.2, 1841

Strecker, Georg, *Der Weg der Gerechtigkeit. Untersuchung zur Theologie des Matthäus,* FRLANT 82, [3]1971

Theissen, Gerd and Merz, Annette, *The Historical Jesus. A Comprehensive Guide,* 1998

Trillhaas, Wolfgang, *Dogmatik,* [3]1972

Türcke, Christoph, *Kassensturz. Zur Lage der Theologie,* 1992

Usener, Hermann, 'Geburt und Kindheit Christi', ZNW 4, 1903, 1–21

Verweyen, Hansjürgen, 'Mariologie als Befreiung. Lk 1, 26–45.56 im Kontext', ZKTh 105, 1983, 168–83

Verweyen, Hansjürgen, *Der Weltkatechismus: Therapie oder Symptom einer kranken Kirche?,* 1993

Vielhauer, Philipp, *Geschichte der urchristlichen Literatur. Einleitung in das Neue Testament, die Apokryphen und die Apostolischen Väter,* 1975

Wex, Marianne, *Parthenogenese heute. Von der Urkraft der Frau, aus sich selbst heraus zu gebären, ohne Beteiligung eines zweiten Geschlechts*, 1992